America and the Future of Theology

America

and the

Future of Theology

Edited by

William A. Beardslee

The Westminster Press · Philadelphia

LIBRARY OF CONGRESS CATALOG CARD NO. 67-11861

PUBLISHED BY THE WESTMINSTER PRESS®

PHILADELPHIA, PENNSYLVANIA

PRINTED IN THE UNITED STATES OF AMERICA

CONTENTS

CONTRIBUTORS

Thomas J. J. Altizer is Associate Professor of Religion, Emory University.

William A. Beardslee is Professor of Religion, Emory University.

William A. Christian is Professor of Religious Studies and Fellow of Timothy Dwight College, Yale University.

Frederick Ferré is Associate Professor of Philosophy and Chairman of the Department of Philosophy, Dickinson College.

Shirley C. Guthrie, Jr., is Professor of Systematic Theology, Columbia Theological Seminary.

Walter Harrelson is Professor of Old Testament and Chairman of the Department of Religion in the Graduate School, Vanderbilt University.

Stanley R. Hopper is Dean of the Graduate School and Professor of Philosophy and Letters, Drew University.

Joseph A. Johnson, Jr., is Bishop of the Fourth Episcopal District of the Christian Methodist Episcopal Church. Prior to his election in 1966 he was Professor of New Testament and Chairman of the Committee on Graduate Studies, Interdenominational Theological Center.

Creighton Lacy is Professor of World Christianity, The Divinity School, Duke University.

Charles H. Long is Associate Professor of History of Religions, The University of Chicago.

Jules Laurence Moreau is Professor of Church History, Seabury-Western Theological Seminary.

Talcott Parsons is Professor of Sociology, Harvard University.

The Very Rev. Bernardin J. Patterson, O.S.B., is Superior of St. Maur's Priory and President of St. Maur's Theological Seminary.

Richard L. Rubenstein is Director of the B'nai B'rith Hillel Foundation and University Chaplain to Jewish Students at the University of Pittsburgh, where he is also Charles L. Merrill Lecturer in the Humanities.

Roger L. Shinn is Dean of Instruction and William E. Dodge, Jr., Professor of Applied Christianity, Union Theological Seminary.

Oliver Read Whitley is Professor of Sociology of Religion, The Iliff School of Theology.

INTRODUCTION

William A. Beardslee

Out of the ghetto! American theologians are responding to this cry. The future of theology lies in a deeper interaction with the contemporary world, and the essays presented here show some of the directions which theology is now taking as it engages in this interaction.

The theologian who "comes out of the ghetto" of religious isolation does not have a very comfortable time of it. He is told that his language does not mean anything, that his social vision is no different from that of the nonbeliever, that the time has passed when we can speak of God; one could extend the list. The theologian is, in short, faced with the question whether he has anything distinctive to say that could not be said as well or better by other interpreters of the meaning of human existence. No expression of faith can be exempted from criticism, reevaluation, and reformulation if the dialogue with the contemporary world is taken seriously.

More accurately, the theologian himself is—or must be—a modern man, so that the encounter does not come toward him from the world outside, but from within his own world. The meeting with the modern world, including its questions about traditional faith, is part of the life of faith itself and of the clarification of faith that we call theology. Theologians also live in a community of faith and are responsible for interpreting the heritage that is given to them. It is not their task to create faith, but to witness as faithful men. This collection of studies centers on the new perspectives and on the questions with which a contemporary faith must grapple. It shows many lines of connection to the established and traditional ways of expressing faith, but it does not systematically try to relate the new perspectives and questions to the various theological traditions. It is, nonetheless, the point of these studies that this must be done and can be done. We believe that the issues raised here are relevant to a wide variety of theological positions. The authors represent predominantly Protestant views, though both a Roman Catholic and a Jewish spokesman appear in the collection.

The emphasis on *American* theology is intended as an effort at better understanding of our own situation, not as a competitive or chauvinistic venture. The extensive use of British and European thinkers, even by those authors who are most self-consciously concerned with America, shows that the scrutiny of American theological creativity is not intended in any spirit of theological isolation. It may be hoped that this collection will show some points where American thinkers can most effectively contribute to the international theological conversation.

The American context may be understood more broadly, in terms of a vision of the whole meaning of American culture and society (as in Thomas J. J. Altizer's essay), or more narrowly, in terms of the particular intellectual traditions and resources which are available and congenial to the American scholarly scene (as in Jules Laurence Moreau's essay). Obviously, these two perspectives overlap (as in Talcott Parsons' chapter), yet there is a considerable difference between trying to offer a whole new symbolic grasp of human existence arising from the present experience of man, and in particular of American man, and identifying an active and viable intellectual development which is becoming an important theological resource.

Thomas J. J. Altizer's essay, "Theology and the Contemporary Sensibility," most directly and with startling imaginative power attempts to use the vision of America as a model for a new

grasp of Christian faith. In his view, "America," freshly understood, may become a paradigmatic symbol of the hope of contemporary Christianity. The symbolic hope that America represents finds its meaning precisely in America's lack of roots in
the past, which makes it possible through this symbol to envision
a total dialectical inversion of traditional faith, in which the
transcendent becomes wholly immanent. His bold, radical Christian vision is judged a fair assessment of the actual situation of
faith in many respects by Richard L. Rubenstein, who, however,
shows how a Jewish theologian could not accept the Christian
framework within which Altizer works; and Rubenstein looks for
a sobering "Europeanization" of American hope. While sympa-
thetic to the acute theological crisis posed by the American
reality, Charles H. Long feels that Altizer is portraying the same
pattern of American naïveté in his eschatological theology.

The other essayists attempt less drastic reconception, both of
the theological task and of the American situation. Jules Laurence
Moreau sets forth some of the difficult questions raised for theology by the analysis of language—a philosophical inquiry now
widely pursued by American philosophers, though by no means
American in origin. Moreau offers a comprehensive sketch of
the meaning of analytic philosophy for theology, and concludes
that it is possible for theological statements to have cognitive
meaning. He is criticized from somewhat opposite sides by
Joseph A. Johnson, Jr., who questions the adequacy of a purely
verbal concept of communication to do justice to the richness
of personal meaning in the encounter of faith, and by Frederick
Ferré, who probes Moreau's presentation of the problem of "verification" with the aim of achieving greater clarity and rigor.

William A. Christian next presents another philosophical
movement that is particularly at home in America—the Whiteheadian philosophy. Christian defends the ontological quest
against its many critics, and shows how the venture of restating
Christian affirmations in Whiteheadian categories may be significant because the Whiteheadian categoreal scheme is more
appropriate to the dynamic, historical Christian faith than are

many of the other ontologies with which Christian theology has been combined. Stanley R. Hopper, in reply, finds that Whitehead's thought, as a genuinely modern vision of the world, requires an even more drastic reconception of faith than Professor Christian proposes. He probes the implications of Whitehead's turning away from any fixed absolute toward creative advance, and of Whitehead's stress on the aesthetic as the central mode of approach to reality. Shirley C. Guthrie emphasizes the political-ethical thrust of Christian faith, but grants that once it is recognized that faith must *begin* its understanding of itself by facing the actual political-ethical world, it may rightly be further clarified by recourse to metaphysics.

Talcott Parsons then sets forth an interpretation of the possibilities of interaction between social science and theology. Perhaps more clearly here than elsewhere we see a theme which runs through most of the essays: that theology from its own distinctive point of view is speaking about the same things that secular disciplines discuss. Parsons works out the implications of this view with respect to social science and theology, showing how the newer social-psychological insights into factors which determine man's behavior are absolutely necessary to any discussion of his freedom, and pointing to several lines of theological rethinking suggested by social science. In balance, Talcott Parsons stands squarely with those who see great possibilities of good in the newer understandings of deterministic factors in human life, though he does not discount the dangers. Walter Harrelson, in his comment, points out how modern Biblical study has uncovered a view of man which, in its "nonreligious" emphasis and in its faith that the world is the realm of God's activity, in many ways parallels the newer secular insights, and he holds that Biblical faith need not be threatened by modern social science. Oliver Read Whitley, directing his comments to Talcott Parson's methodology, questions him at several points, notably with the query whether Parsons' emphasis on structure does not lead him to underestimate, in his theoretical analysis, the possibility of there being a "tyranny of order."

Roger L. Shinn addresses the question of "The Public Responsibility of Theology," taking this question in its broadest sense and giving, within the broader perspective, a central place for responsibility in the field of social ethics. The role of faith in a pluralistic society is one that American Protestant faith, at least, does not yet understand very well, because it has been so long in a dominant position in an only nominally pluralistic society. That the shift from nominal pluralism to actual pluralism does not bring any retreat from public responsibility is the forceful thesis of Roger Shinn. Father Bernardin J. Patterson's comment calls for a more vigorous theological participation in interdisciplinary dialogue, and points toward some of the specific areas where exercise of public responsibility is particularly needed. Creighton Lacy clarifies the meaning of public responsibility, particularly with reference to issues that reach beyond the American scene—Communism and revolutionary change in Asia and Africa—thus closing the collection on a note that reminds the reader of the impossibility of thinking about American theology in isolation from the rest of the world.

If one were to hazard a comment about what directions emerge from the collection, it would appear that two rather different directions do emerge. One is the attempt at major reconception of the whole framework of Christian theology. The radical theology of Thomas J. J. Altizer and the Whiteheadian theology proposed by William A. Christian both represent enterprises of this sort. The other direction is the turning away from a total vision to work concretely at a specific and definable segment of the overall task. One gains the impression that this latter enterprise is more characteristic of the current theological scene as a whole, and the more modest tasks of redefining and reexamining smaller parts of the theological tradition may well occupy the attention of most theologians for some time to come. Such work has immense vigor and importance. At the same time it is heartening to find the other theological task, that of major reconception, boldly under way.

These papers result from a conference held at Emory University in November, 1965, and jointly sponsored by Columbia Theological Seminary, Emory University's Graduate Division of Religion, the Interdenominational Theological Center, and The Westminster Press. To its planning and execution many persons contributed; here only the work of the planning committee can be noted: S. Barton Babbage and Neely D. McCarter of Columbia Theological Seminary, William Mallard of Emory University, and Melvin H. Watson and Ralph L. Williamson of the Interdenominational Theological Center, along with the editor, participated in planning the program. The views of the speakers, of course, are not necessarily those of the institutions sponsoring the conference. The deepest appreciation is hereby expressed to those who made the conference possible: President J. McDowell Richards of Columbia Theological Seminary, Dean Charles T. Lester of the Graduate School of Emory University, President Harry V. Richardson of the Interdenominational Theological Center, and the staff of The Westminster Press. We are indebted to Mrs. Margaret Westbrook and to James H. LaFon for careful work in the preparation of the conference and of the typescript.

I

THEOLOGY AND THE

CONTEMPORARY SENSIBILITY

Thomas J. J. Altizer

I

At a time when the image of America threatens to pass into the very opposite of its original promise, and when American society would appear to be moving into an ultimate phase of that alienation, anomie, and dehumanization which is the fruit of existence in a highly technological and urban culture, we must face the urgent task of discovering the contemporary meaning of the American destiny. However, we must not simply accept at face value the given reality of America in our day; we must not mistake the seeming dominance of the mass, impersonal, public domain as the true body of America; nor may we allow the revolutionary American idea of freedom to be appropriated by those spokesmen who would invert it into a new law of repression. Recognizing that truth is always other than a deceptive appearance, we must search for the true identity of America in a source beyond that of its public consciousness. Theologically considered, and in the perspective of America's original Christian roots, we must be in quest of a meaning of America that goes beyond and even negates all that repressive reality of the present which restricts and confines the human hand and face. Such a meaning must be both redemptive and apocalyptic, redemptive in the sense of America's original promise of a universal historical liberation of humanity, and apocalyptic in the sense of the Christian hope in a new and final victory of the Kingdom of God.

Perhaps the clearest spokesman for the hope originally inspired by America is William Blake, whose poem *America*, which was first engraved in 1793, was Blake's first fully prophetic work of art, and it marks an attempt to reconceive the American Revolution as a new historical reality that has already embarked upon a sweeping transformation of all previous history. At the same time it apocalyptically envisions America as the spatial point at which Eternity is becoming totally manifest upon the plane of time. The hero of *America* is Orc, a symbolical figure embodying the primordial and now revolutionary fire of passion, a cosmic rebel who will later be transposed by Blake into Los, or the "Human Imagination." As the poem opens, morning dawns, the graves burst open, and the suddenly released souls of enchained men sing:

> . . . "The Sun has left his blackness & has found a fresher morning,
> And the fair Moon rejoices in the clear & cloudless night;
> For Empire is no more, and now the Lion & Wolf shall cease."   (*America* 6:13–15.)

Here we see Blake employing Christian apocalyptic imagery along with Messianic imagery from The Book of Isaiah in such a way as to merge a prophetic and an apocalyptic vision. Immediately, Orc appears, and he is inevitably greeted by the agents of political and moral tyranny as a blasphemous Demon, Antichrist, lover of wild rebellion, and transgressor of God's Law. Orc then responds with a violent assault upon the religion inspired by the God who is the transcendent ground of repression:

> "The times are ended; shadows pass, the morning 'gins to break;
> The fiery joy, that Urizen perverted to ten commands,
> What night he led the starry hosts thro' the wide wilderness,
> That stony law I stamp to dust; and scatter religion abroad
> To the four winds as a torn book, & none shall gather the leaves."   (*America* 8:1–6.)

Urizen is Blake's symbol of the Christian God or the transcendent Creator, whom Blake proclaims to be the ultimate source of all tyranny and repression, and *America* not only records Blake's first full vision of the Christian God as Urizen, but it also unveils the dawning apocalyptic event of the death of God.

In this poem, Orc *is* America, for Blake sees the true America as a resurrected passion awakening to reverse the sleep of history and to annihilate the iron laws of repression. The red fires of America's rebellion rage with fury, reducing tyranny's armies to a naked multitude, deforming the ancient heavens, opening the doors of marriage, and driving all priests into "reptile coverts" where they hide from the fires of Orc, thereby leaving the females naked and glowing with the "lusts of youth." If Orc is "ruddy"—red being the color of the fiery joy of passion and revolution—then Urizen now appears in a form that is white and icy:

> Over the hills, the vales, the cities, rage the red flames
> fierce:
> The Heavens melted from north to south; and Urizen, who
> sat
> Above all heavens, in thunders wrap'd, emerg'd his leprous
> head
> From out his holy shrine, his tears in deluge piteous
> Falling into the deep sublime; flag'd with grey-brow'd
> snows
> And thunderous visages, his jealous wings wav'd over the
> deep;
> Weeping in dismal howling woe, he dark descended,
> howling
> Around the smitten bands, clothed in tears & trembling,
> shudd'ring cold.
> His stored snows he poured forth, and his icy magazines
> He open'd on the deep, and on the Atlantic sea white
> shiv'ring
> Leprous his limbs, all over white, and hoary was his
> visage,
> Weeping in dismal howlings before the stern Americans.
> (*America* 16:1–12.)

Notice that the fires of Orc or America renew the primordial joy which Urizen had perverted into the Decalogue; this renewal consumes all moral laws and religion, resurrects the holy life of youthful "lust," and melts the heavens hiding Urizen from earth. Only as a consequence of this cosmic reversal does Urizen appear in his white and icy form: weeping and trembling he then descends to earth, and pours his "stored snows" upon the sea of time and space.

In this poem Blake directs his apocalyptic imagery to an initial vision of the dissolution of that chaos which is the seer's name for a fallen cosmos, and fragmentary as his prophetic vision is in this its earliest form, it succeeds marvelously in revealing the polar union between the distant Urizen and an inverted world. But the "Mystery" of Urizen is unveiled in the context of an eschatological end: only through a final reversal of a fallen time and space does Urizen lose his numinous and transcendent form and return to a now liberated humanity in the naked condition of his dying state. It must be confessed that the prophecy of *America* was premature for a prophet who had yet to undergo his deepest encounter with Urizen or the Christian God. At this point Blake had only taken his first real step in the direction of "naming" God as Satan, a "naming" that transformed both Blake and his work. Nevertheless, Blake already sees that the death of God is an eschatological event which cannot be dissociated from the triumphant dawning of the Apocalypse. While America virtually disappears from his vision during Blake's Joblike wrestling with the Christian God, it returns still bearing an apocalyptic identity in the final stages of his work. In *Jerusalem*, America is identified as the closed "Western Gate" of Albion, or the universal cosmic Man; it is hidden "for a Curse, an Altar of Victims & a Holy Place" (*Jerusalem* 82:29); for the tribes of America must hide until "sweet Jerusalem emanates again into Eternity" (*Jerusalem* 83:60). May we suspect that Blake refrained from employing the symbolic name of America in any vision falling short of the totality of the New Eden? In any case, it is clear that the

late Blake simultaneously associated America with a dark altar
of suffering humanity and a place destined for a cosmic renewal
by an apocalyptic Light.

Blake might well have rejoiced that destiny was soon to give
the world its most awesome vision of the Christian God, and he
certainly would have expressed no surprise if he could have
known that an American artist and seer would create Moby
Dick. If *Moby Dick* is the first symbolical novel, then Ahab
must be acknowledged as the first hero of modern literature
who fully plays a dual historical and mythological role. Ahab
is at once an embodiment of the dark altar of America—he has
made the full transition from "Innocence" to "Experience,"
and his innocence reappears in the novel in the form of Pip only
to be driven mad by Ahab's God—and a hero who plays the
Orcian role of striking through the mask of God. When Starbuck accuses Ahab of madness for seeking vengeance on a
dumb brute, Ahab replies with the never-to-be-forgotten words:

> "All visible objects, man, are but as pasteboard masks. But
> in each event—in the living act, the undoubted deed—
> there, some unknown but still reasoning thing puts forth
> the mouldings of its features from behind the unreasoning
> mask. If man will strike, strike through the mask! How can
> the prisoner reach outside except by thrusting through the
> wall? To me, the white whale is that wall, shoved near to
> me. Sometimes I think there's naught beyond. But 'tis enough.
> He tasks me; he heaps me; I see in him outrageous strength,
> with an inscrutable malice sinewing it. That inscrutable thing
> is chiefly what I hate; and be the white whale agent, or be
> the white whale principal, I will wreak that hate upon him.
> Talk not to me of blasphemy, man; I'd strike the sun if it
> insulted me."

Ahab's Promethean pride is directed to striking off all the
fetters that bind suffering humanity to a cruel fate, and he
passionately seeks the destruction of the face behind the mask
of Moby Dick, knowing full well that his quest has made of
him a "Curse" and an "Altar." Denying that he is mad, Ahab
insists that he is demoniac: "I am madness maddened! That

wild madness that's only calm to comprehend itself!" Yet the pious Captain Peleg calls Ahab a "grand, ungodly, godlike man," and Ahab must surely have been Melville's personification of the tragic destiny of America.

Can we accept Ahab as a personification of the eschatological destiny of America? *Moby Dick* has no apocalyptic imagery, and significantly enough it is a novel with neither a resolution nor a conclusion, yet its mythical center is set in the context of a modern Western realism, and its nihilistic evocation of a faceless but cosmic evil makes the primordial chaos incarnate in the God who is present upon our horizon. Ahab, who has been burned and scarred by a sacramental worship of the God of fire, knows that "right worship is defiance."

> "I own thy speechless, placeless power; but to the last gasp of my earthquake life will dispute its unconditional, unintegral mastery in me. In the midst of the personified impersonal, a personality stands here. Though but a point at best; whencesoe'er I came; wheresoe'er I go; yet while I earthly live, the queenly personality lives in me, and feels her royal rights. But war is pain, and hate is woe. Come in thy lowest form of love, and I will kneel and kiss thee; but at thy highest, come as mere supernal power; and though thou launchest navies of full-freighted worlds, there's that in here that still remains indifferent. Oh, thou clear spirit, of thy fire thou madest me, and like a true child of fire, I breathe it back to thee."

Like America, Ahab has no real history, except insofar as he has been burned by its fallenness; by standing in the midst of "the personified impersonal" he anticipates a later destiny of America; and, although madness maddened, he greets the dawning apocalyptic "Mystery" of God with the true worship of defiance. As a tragic hero, Ahab has no "choice"; he must seek out and kill Moby Dick—whether he succeeds or not is, of course, another matter. His tragic conflict with the white whale brings upon himself the death that he would inflict upon the whale, and by dying while lashed upon the whale's back he plunges into the sea of chaos and is swallowed up by the sepulcher of God.

II

Apocalyptically envisioned, the Kingdom of God dawns at the end of history; its triumph is inseparable from the disintegration of the old cosmos, and it calls for the reversal of an established law and the collapse of all previous religion. Despite the fact that Jesus' message and ministry were grounded in an eschatological proclamation of the dawning of the Kingdom of God, Christian theology has never been able to assimilate this apocalyptic ground of faith. But we are now living in a time when the whole inherited body of our theological language is disappearing into the past, a new history is dawning in our midst before which theology is increasingly becoming speechless, and America is symbolically and perhaps literally the place at which this revolutionary history has become dominant. Wherever we turn among the great revolutionary prophets of the nineteenth century, whether to Blake, to Hegel, to Dostoevsky, or to Nietzsche, we find that this new historical reality is symbolically associated with the death of God, for only the death of God can make possible the advent of a new humanity. Just as apocalyptic imagery centers upon the defeat of Satan or Antichrist, whose death alone ushers in the victory of the Kingdom of God, so contemporary thought and sensibility is rooted in an absolute negation of God, a negation that already promises to dissolve even the memory of God. We must take due note of the fact that Blake, who was the first Christian poet to create an apocalypse, envisioned the American Revolution as an apocalyptic victory effecting the death of God, for the Blake who dared to name God as Satan identified the transcendent Lord as the ultimate source of alienation and repression. Thus Blake could greet the death of God with the joyous acceptance of faith and was impelled thereby to unveil the divine identity of a dying Satan with the assurance that his death would inaugurate the final triumph of "The Great Humanity Divine." If Melville's Moby Dick is yet another form of the dying God's white and now lifeless body disappearing into the sea of the past, then we must ask if the symbolical meaning of America is not to be theologically identified with an eschatological passage through the death of God.

But what can it mean to speak of the death of God as an eschatological event? First, we must note that the great nineteenth-century revolutionary thinkers conceived the death of God as a historical event: Hegel understood the advent of absolute Spirit to be effected by Spirit's absolute self-negation of its original and transcendent form, a negation whereby Spirit kenotically empties itself and becomes historically incarnate in its own intrinsic other; Kierkegaard conceived of faith as a subjectivity that is the antithetical opposite of objectivity, where objectivity is understood to be a historical reality created by the negation of faith, with the inevitable result that Christianity no longer exists objectively or historically—hence Kierkegaard's final attack upon the Christianity of his day as being exactly the opposite of New Testament Christianity; and Nietzsche proclaimed the death of God as the most important event in history, for modern man's murder of God has for once and for all annihilated every transcendent source of order and meaning and made incarnate the most awesome nothingness imaginable. Each of these thinkers, in their distinctively different ways, believed that history was entering a new era, an era at least as important as that brought on by the birth of human consciousness, and an era so radically different from man's previous history that no historical analogy could illuminate its uniqueness. When the death of God is thus conceived as an actual and final historical event, there can be no waiting for a new epiphany of God in a future historical moment, nor for that matter can there be a longing for a historical moment of the past when God was still present, if only because the actuality of his death has obliterated his presence in all historical time.

Now it is only in the historical situation of the death of God that we can understand Blake's violent attack upon Urizen, Hegel's philosophical judgment that abstract or transcendent Spirit is alien and lifeless, Dostoevsky's rebellion against an absolutely sovereign God, and Nietzsche's passionate assault upon the Christian God as the ground of No-saying and *ressentiment*. Theologically considered, we might say that it is only when God himself has died in his original and primordial form that he can be truly known as the source of alienation and repression, for then he no longer has a living existence as the God who alone is God, and can exist as God only in the bad faith of those who refuse the death of God and cling to his primordial image even at the cost of the negation of life and history. Yet it also follows theologically that a passage through the death of God, at least in the perspective of radical Christianity, makes possible a wholly new form of faith. Thus Blake celebrated the death of God as inaugurating the New Jerusalem, Hegel conceived the self-negation of Spirit as effecting the birth of Spirit in self-consciousness, Dostoevsky's Kirillov reaches "man-godhood" by reversing God-manhood, and Nietzsche proclaimed the death of God as the portal through which to pass to the total Yes-saying of Dionysian faith. Moreover, these new forms of faith may be seen to have an apocalyptic form: the new humanity that they proclaim dawns only at the end of all that we have known as history; its triumph is inseparable from the disintegration of the cosmos created by historical man, and it calls for the reversal of all moral law and the collapse of all historical religion. Ironically enough, it is the apocalyptic form of this new and revolutionary faith which has done most to make it appear anti-Christian. The theologian has all too naturally cried "Anti-Christ" in the presence of this vision, quite rightly judging its call to total redemption to be a negation or inversion of historical Christianity—just as the revolutionary modern seer has identified the God of ecclesiastical or historical Christianity as Satan or Antichrist or an abstract and impassive Nothing.

If we accept Blake, Hegel, Dostoevsky, and Nietzsche as the

primary prophetic spokesmen of the death of God, then we must come to understand the death of God as a Christian event, as an ultimate but consistent consequence of an original and radical Christianity. When the late Blake inscribed his Laocoön engraving with the words, "God is Jesus," he was giving a concise if cryptic expression to his vision in *Milton* and *Jerusalem* that Jesus is the "seventh eye of God," for God has come and freely died in Jesus. This radical Christian faith in the total presence of God in Jesus is also found in Hegel, who believed that, in the incarnation, Spirit kenotically emptied itself of its original divine substance and became self-consciousness. Even Nietzsche declared in *The Antichrist* that the gospel of ecclesiastical Christianity is the opposite of that which Jesus had lived, therefore it is an "ill tidings" or a *dysangel*, for Jesus had proclaimed that any distance separating God and man is abolished, and now grace or blessedness is the only reality. Both Nietzsche's portrait of Zarathustra and his vision of Eternal Recurrence are dialectical inversions of the ecclesiastical dogmas of Christ and the Kingdom of God, but they are intended to effect a negation of the church's negation of Jesus, and to resurrect in a new and universal form Jesus' reversal of the No-saying of religion. The "Experience" that Blake envisioned as the dialectical contrary of "Innocence," the full actuality *(Wirklichkeit)* that Hegel knew to be the destiny of Spirit, the Yes-saying to life, the body, and the earth that Nietzsche opposed to all No-saying—all are expressions of a uniquely Christian faith in a Word that has fully and finally become flesh. Not until the disintegration of Christendom did the death of God become realized or actualized historically, but, from the point of view of radical faith, this is because ecclesiastical Christianity sealed Jesus in his tomb by resurrecting him in the form of an exalted and transcendent Lord, thereby negating the true and underlying meaning of the incarnation and the crucifixion. Once ecclesiastical or historical Christianity has itself been negated, then the incarnation will decisively and historically become manifest as the death of God in Jesus, for the God who *is* Jesus has passed through an ultimate and final self-negation in becoming all in all.

III

It would appear that Blake's was the first prophetic voice to declare or to envision the death of God (as we have seen, this occurred in 1793), and we must return to the fact that Blake then envisioned the death of Urizen as an apocalyptic event effected or unveiled by the advent of the American Revolution. How startling it must seem to the contemporary American that a revolutionary European could think of America as the dawning of a new aeon of the future! But Blake was not alone at this point among his European compeers, and even the late Hegel could say in his lectures on the philosophy of history that "America is the land of the future; in it, in the time lying before us . . . the significance of world history will be revealed." We Americans must realize that the true America is the land of the future and not the literal nation about us, and it is a land that will only realize its destiny by passing through all which we now know as past. Above all, America is called freely to accept and will the death of God, to join Ahab in his murderous hunt for the white whale, for even if the American becomes "madness maddened," he must move through the chaos of our disintegrating history to reach an apocalyptic goal. Nothing less than an apocalyptic destiny can be a consequence of a total epiphany of the death of God, for either we will be drowned in that nihilistic "night" foreseen by Nietzsche as the destiny of our century or we will pass through this rebirth of the primordial chaos to the dawn of a new and glorious Jerusalem.

Perhaps the one quality clearly distinguishing the American consciousness is a detachment from the past, or at least a detachment from what the European consciousness knows as past, for as Heidegger has remarked, metaphysically speaking, America and Russia are the same, insofar as "time as history" has vanished from human life. We may observe something of the meaning of this quality by noting the almost invariable hostility of the contemporary European intellectual toward our present and its apparent historical future, whereas the distinctively American thinker tends to affirm the future, and to hope for a new form of the human hand and face. Few contemporary Americans can immediately associate a living moment with a moment of the past; hence we tend to be in quest of a new form of existence in a future which is not simply an extension of the present, but rather a future shattering all that given reality which is static and unmoving in our present. Indeed, the time has at long last come for America to assume a creative theological vocation, a vocation previously denied it, for America lacks those deep roots in the past which have thus far been an essential presupposition of theological creativity. While the established forms of Christian theology have largely been given to the priestly goal of converging the present and the past, a true theological renewal will seek a rebirth of theology in a new form by seeking a convergence of the present and the future. Now theology is called to die of its old self, to cast aside its previous body, seeking a language substantially if not wholly different from its previous speech, if only to give birth to a theological language that can truly speak in our present. Moreover, if theology is to evolve to language that can speak in the presence of our future, it must recover an eschatological form, a form transposing the original Christian apocalyptic proclamation so that it may be open to a new and revolutionary future.

Recognizing that our historical present is progressively losing its ground in the past, we cannot fail to note that our inherited theological language is increasingly becoming empty and silent, as the traditional Word of faith can now speak only in those diminishing pockets of our history that are isolated from the actuality of the present. Only by negating its inherited form will theology evolve to a new and contemporary language, for to the extent that theology remains bound to its established and given identity, it will be reduced to little more than an echo of its once living voice. We must not imagine, however, that the substance or the deposit of Christian theology is unchanging, with the reassuring corollary that a new theology will simply adopt a new style or an updated dress. Already the time has passed when the responsible theologian could believe that it is still possible to express the established doctrines of faith in a language meaningful to the contemporary sensibility, and while many of our most influential theologians now seem to believe that the resolution of this problem lies in abandoning dogmatic for kerygmatic theology, the simple fact remains that the event of proclamation can only be a deceptive mirage if there is a speaker but no Word, an act of proclamation but no Word proclaimed. Our·problem as theologians is to unveil a new form of the Word or, rather, to engage in a radical reconstruction of the whole form and language of theology so as to make possible a living and contemporary theology, for only on the basis of a comprehensive and thoroughgoing rethinking of theology can a Word appearing in our history become thinkable as faith. Yet theology will continue to remain closed to our present if it remains bound to the Word of its own past; so long as it speaks the language of a past and now long distant form of faith, its speech will necessarily be hollow and unreal. Not until theology moves through a radical self-negation, thereby undergoing a metamorphosis into a new form, will it be able to meet the challenge of our present.

When we become conscious of the challenge of our theological situation in the perspective of an apocalyptic form of faith, we might well take due note of the crucial movement in apocalyptic faith: a movement from old to new in the context of an imminent collapse of the old cosmos as a new aeon dawns in such a way as to shatter the old, and only on the basis of an interior participation in such a cosmic transfiguration can an apocalyptic faith become actualized and real. However, a faith that is both Christian and apocalyptic cannot seek an eschatological End which will be a repetition of the primordial Beginning. In this form, apocalyptic faith shares the universal religious quest for an original and primordial sacred, thereby losing the forward movement of the incarnation, and inverting the truly future eschatological aeon into the original form of God before the creation. As opposed to the purely religious movement of involution and return, a Christian expression of apocalyptic faith must move into the future by negating the past, for apart from a total negation of the power of the past there can be no movement into an eschatological future. Consequently, the inherent movement and direction of the incarnate Word demands that it move into the future by negating the past. Furthermore, an incarnate Word cannot continue to be incarnate apart from a continual process of negating its own past expressions, of moving beyond its own particular expressions into an ever more total and universal epiphany in history. If this movement is actual and real, that is to say if it is a genuine movement from a real past to a real future, then it must be a forward-moving process of self-negation or self-transformation, wherein the Word negates its past to realize its future. Not until the incarnate Word has moved through a total negation of its original and primordial form can it realize its own eschatological future and thereby reach a truly apocalyptic consummation.

The decisive question before the contemporary Christian is whether or not he will be able to open himself to the full actuality of our history, giving himself to the moment before us with the stance of faith, and meeting that moment with the assurance that it must finally embody an epiphany of a kenotic and incarnate Word. No longer can the Christian find security in an absolutely sovereign God who exercises·a beneficent and providential dominion over the world. That God has disappeared from view or, rather, he is visible in our history only insofar as he has become alien and lifeless, thereby appearing as the God of an irrecoverable past or an inhuman present. If ours is in some sense an apocalyptic situation, a point standing midway between two completely different forms of the world, can we conceive of a Christian understanding of God that would apprehend God as the primordial ground of the old aeon or the original form of the world? Once granted that faith can no longer truly know God in the present, or that the God who appears in our present is in no sense a source of redemption and life, then theology must resolutely confine the Christian name of God to the past, and wholly refrain from proclaiming his redemptive presence in our historical present. Yet if the Christian God has become a God of the past, and our past is disintegrating under the impact of a revolutionary future, then theology must posit God as the ultimate source of a world or history that is now passing away. Just as a primitive Christian faith could know the dawning of the Kingdom of God in the heart of darkness, and give itself to an absolute negation of that darkness as the way to the light and life of Christ, so a contemporary Christian faith must know our darkness as the tomb of the primordial God who has negated himself in Christ, and pass through the darkness of a dying God to a new and apocalyptic epiphany of Christ. Indeed, a Christian passage through the death of God would make possible a recovery of the forward movement of apocalyptic faith and a rebirth of faith itself in a transfigured yet consistently eschatological form.

IV

Let us once again return to the image of America as it appears in Blake's *America* and the whaling voyage of Melville's *Moby Dick*. When Urizen falls weeping from heaven at the end of *America*, he is manifest in a white and icy form, and dies while pouring his snows upon the "deep." Remembering Dante's image of Satan or Dis as a lifeless and impassive figure encrusted in ice, we might well associate Urizen's icy frozenness with a Satanic epiphany, and then conceive the pouring of his snows as the final negation or emptying of the original body of God, with the result that God now appears in the empty or nihilistic form of Satan. The whiteness of Urizen is both ·the death shroud of the now naked Creator and the symbol of a seemingly absolute and certainly life-destroying power. In a parallel manner, Moby Dick's whiteness embodies a cosmic evil lying behind and beneath the creation, while simultaneously evoking the sacred purity of the Holy Spirit. Melville says that whiteness is the "very veil" of the Christian God, but this most potent symbol of the Spirit is also the "intensifying agent" in things the most appalling to mankind:

> Is it that by its indefiniteness it shadows forth the heartless voids and immensities of the universe, and thus stabs us from behind with the thought of annihilation, when beholding the white depths of the milky way? Or is it, that as in essence whiteness is not so much a color as the visible absence of color, and at the same time the concrete of all colors; is it for these reasons that there is such a dumb blankness, full of meaning, in a wide landscape of snows— a colorless, all-color of atheism from which we shrink? And when we consider that . . . all other earthly hues . . . are but subtle deceits, not actually inherent in substances, but only laid on from without; so that all deified Nature absolutely paints like the harlot, whose allurements cover nothing but the charnel-house within; and when we proceed further, and consider that the mystical cosmetic which produces every one of her hues, the great principle of light, for ever remains white or colorless in itself, and if operating without medium upon matter, would touch all objects, even tulips and roses, with its own blank tinge—pondering all this, the palsied universe lies before us as a leper.

Only Ahab's fiery hunt unveils this meaning of the whiteness of the whale, but through Ahab we can know the totality of an old aeon as finally existing in the image of its now Satanic Creator, and also know Moby Dick as the primordial "principle of light" who now reveals Himself in his final form as lifeless or colorless himself.

Although Blake's *America* has had little effect upon the American consciousness, *Moby Dick* has almost assumed the status of an American epic, and Ahab's heroic hunt for the white whale is increasingly becoming an image of America's destiny. Reversing the order of their composition, we might imagine *America*

as an apocalyptic resolution of Melville's unfinished novel. Then
we might read the following lines as occurring after Moby
Dick disappears into the mysterious deeps:

> "The times are ended; shadows pass, the morning 'gins to
> break;
> The fiery joy, that Urizen perverted to ten commands,
> What night he led the starry hosts thro' the wide wilderness,
> That stony law I stamp to dust; and scatter religion abroad
> To the four winds as a torn book, & none shall gather
> the leaves."

The speaker of these lines could only be an America who has
not only freely passed through the death of God, but who has
also joined Ahab in becoming the murderer of God, breathing
God's fire back into the body of a dying Satan, so that his white
and leprous body might undergo a cataclysmic destruction, thus
finally annihilating every memory and image of a "palsied universe." When *Moby Dick* is read in the context of *America*,
Ahab's mad quest for the white whale can be seen as faith's
response to the death of God, wherein the man of faith becomes
the murderer of God so as to make possible a historical actualization of God's death in Jesus, and thus an apocalyptic consummation of God's original self-sacrifice or self-negation. Consequently, the Christian who truly and finally wills God's death
will realize the apocalyptic promise of those primary words,
"God *is* love," for he will actualize in a new and universal
humanity that New Eden envisioned by Blake in *Jerusalem:*

> Jesus said: "Wouldest thou love one who never died
> For thee, or ever die for one who had not died for thee?
> And if God dieth not for Man & giveth not himself
> Eternally for Man, Man could not exist; for Man is Love
> As God is Love: every kindness to another is a little Death
> In the Divine Image, nor can Man exist but by Brotherhood."

I A

THOMAS ALTIZER'S APOCALYPSE

Richard L. Rubenstein

I am delighted for this opportunity to respond to Dr. Altizer's work, which I have admired, and to speak on the issue of the "death of God" theology. I would like to state at the outset that I believe that what these theologians are saying about the death of God *as a cultural event* is irrefutable. I start with this premise. I do not like to use the phrase "God is dead" for the reason already suggested by Dr. Altizer: in some sense this symbolism is specifically Christian. In Christianity, the Christ who is both God and man dies and in some versions of Christianity he is also resurrected. I hesitate to use the term "death of God" because I do not want to associate myself with an exclusively Christian symbol arising originally out of the crucifixion tradition. I cannot. As a Jewish theologian, Jesus as a man or Jesus as the Christ has absolutely no significance for me. I cannot even say that he was a great teacher because we really don't regard him as such. Nevertheless, what Hegel, Nietzsche, and Dostoevsky understood by the death of God— the absence of any sense of meaning, direction, or value derived from a transcendent theistic source—is certainly an accurate description of the way we experience the world.

I also welcome the "death of God" theologians because I believe they start with the real spiritual problems of the twentieth century. They begin where twentieth-century man finds himself.

They attempt to offer theological insight concerning human existence in the twentieth century as it really is.

Nevertheless, while I believe that the death of God is a cultural fact, I cannot share the apocalyptic enthusiasm that Professor Altizer seems to attach to this event. As I read Dr. Altizer's paper, I was reminded of Paul Tillich's comment in *The Courage to Be* that the God of theism is dead and deserved to die because he was an enemy of human freedom. I also thought of something that Jean-Paul Sartre has said repeatedly. For Sartre, there is no doubt that God *is* dead. According to Sartre, we live in a universe that is utterly devoid of meaning and hope. We are condemned to be free. While Dr. Altizer sees the death of God as liberation and apocalyptic promise, Sartre, I think, more correctly and with deeper insight, understands this event in terms of condemnation and anguish.

This problem was already understood by Søren Kierkegaard, who turned away in radical fright from that which Professor Altizer takes as a portent of apocalyptic liberation. Kierkegaard understood that the death of God meant absolute despair and hopelessness. He could not accept this. After he had pushed the negation of Christian belief to the dialectic extreme of absolute despair and absolute hopelessness, he turned and made the leap to the Christ. What is important in Kierkegaard is not necessarily his leap, but his understanding that funerals are sad events —even the funeral of God. Albert Camus has commented in his *The Myth of Sisyphus* on Kierkegaard's dialectic turning away from despair toward faith. Camus accepts Kierkegaard's either/or of faith or ultimate despair, but sees no way of avoiding a life without hope. I do not believe it is necessary to live entirely in the dimension of despair. Nevertheless, although I can accept the proclamation of the death of God, I cannot accept the apocalyptic enthusiasm that comes out of it.

One twentieth-century prophet of the death of God is, I find, strikingly absent from Professor Altizer's thought, and from the list that he has given us. He is the one who has suggested that religion actually begins with the death of God, the first object of human criminality. This is, of course, the Sigmund Freud of *Totem and Taboo* and *Moses and Monotheism*. What is significant about *Totem and Taboo* and *Moses and Monotheism* is not whether religion actually began with the brothers of the primal horde cannibalistically consuming the father, but that man's sense of guilt and his involvement in civilization is partly due to his being appalled by his own parricidal inclinations.

Freud's myth is instructive, because it suggests the futility of seeking an end to repression and limitation in the death of God as Professor Altizer would do. The sons murder the father because he has access to the women of the primal horde. In order to possess them, they murder the father. But once the deed was done, they realized that they were bound to destroy each other unless they arranged some instrumentality whereby social cohesiveness would not be threatened by sexual competitiveness. According to Freud, this was accomplished when the sons instituted the law of exogamy. Those who had participated in the crime were compelled to go outside of the tribe to find their mates. Having murdered the father for withholding the females of the horde, they then prevented themselves from possessing the very same wives and daughters just as the father had done. They discovered that the father was not the author of repression and limit. Reality itself demands limit and discipline whether there is a God or not.

I am distrustful of all Promethean proclamations of freedom that come with the death of God. I think Albert Camus understood this when he suggested that Christianity is guilty of the sin of *hubris*. As Martin P. Nilsson has suggested, *hubris* is not the sin of overweening pride but of taking upon oneself more in the order of being than one has a right to. Inevitably, *hubris* is followed by nemesis. The scales are righted. The harmony of things is restored. Anaxagoras saw all existence as a kind of *hubris*, and death as the payment by which we render account. Insofar as the primary parsimony of nature is violated by life itself, we are in a sense taking upon ourselves more in the order of being than we have a right to. Death is a restoration of the disturbed harmony. Camus insists that men must take seriously the old Greek insights about *hubris* and *nemesis*. The idea of an apocalyptic humanity, overreaching itself in a new liberation, is an illusion. It is an attempt to seek for the impossible: a new aeon, a new being, a new heaven, and a new earth.

I feel strangely as if Dr. Altizer and I are Christian and Pharisee in the first century all over again. Incidentally, when I say Pharisee, I simply mean rabbi because all rabbis are of the Pharisaic school. Basically, what was the issue between them? Jesus represented the promise of a new beginning, a fulfillment, a radical change in man's tragic and broken condition. The sad answer of the rabbis was that nothing new has happened. The world in its sadness goes on. The rabbis did not recognize any "good news." In another context, Dostoevsky's Grand Inquisitor was to have more faith in the ongoing institutions to which he had become accustomed than in the radical insecurity of the Christ returned to earth with the promise of a new start for mankind. There is tragic resignation in the refusal to accept novelty and hopefulness. Unfortunately, it is inevitable. The Pharisees and the early Christians saw the problem in terms of whether God had sent his anointed thus beginning a new hope for mankind. One said, "Yes, he has come. The new aeon has begun." The other said, "No, he has not. Things are no different today than they were yesterday." Today, both Dr. Altizer and I stand in the time of the "death of God," and we find that Christian and Jew are still arguing about the new being and the new aeon. The Christian hopefully proclaims the new aeon, and the Jew sadly says: "Would that it were so. Would that there were less evil. Would that there were less human vice. Would that the complexities of even the lusts which we are now free to express were less tragic than they are. But unfortunately the complex, tragic nature of man goes on."

I agree with Albert Camus when he suggests that of all the evils in Pandora's box none was so great as hope. I reject ultimate hope completely. I don't mean that I cannot hope that tomorrow I will have a good day or that in the years ahead I

may enjoy a measure of fulfillment in my life. I reject hope in
the sense that I believe that out of nothingness we have come
and to nothingness we will return. This is our ultimate situation.
I find myself drawn to the "death of God" theologians. If I
have to choose sides, I'll choose my sides with them, because then
radical recognition of God's absence as a cultural fact offers
the only basis for theological speculation in our time. Nevertheless, I don't like to use the words "death of God"—I've joked
about this with my students, though with serious intent. They
have said, "Well, are you a 'death of God' theologian or not?"
My answer is, "I am a 'holy Nothingness' theologian."

Let me attempt to suggest an alternative myth to the one
implicit in what Dr. Altizer is saying. It's a myth that Dr. Altizer will undoubtedly recognize with his understanding of mysticism and eschatology. That is the myth of Lurianic Kabbalism.
Isaac Luria (d. 1572) was a Jewish mystic in the sixteenth century. After the catastrophes of Spanish Jewish life and the ex-
pulsion of the Jews in 1492, he developed a radical theory of
creation. According to Luria, the world came into being when
God created it *ex nihilo*, out of nothingness. This nothingness was
not exterior to God. God created the world out of *his own
nothingness* through an act of self-diminution not unrelated
to Hegel's idea of God kenotically emptying himself to which
Dr. Altizer alludes. Whatever has been created out of God's
nothingness is caught in a dialectic dilemma from which it can
never escape. Insofar as it is aware of its true origin in the
divine nothingness—no-thing-ness would be better than nothingness—it yearns to return to its source. Insofar as it desires to
maintain its separate identity, it is in alienation, separated from
God's nothingness. According to Luria, all existence is in an
unavoidable dialectic conflict between the tendency toward self-
maintenance and the yearning to return to the nothingness that
is our true origin and our real essence. Eventually, of course,
God's nothingness is victorious. With the self-division of God, in
Luria as in Hegel, negation comes into existence. The price paid
for creation is negation. And negation brings evil in its train.

That does not mean creation is evil; it does mean that part of creation is inevitably evil and there is, as Melville understood, a demonic side to God himself. God cannot create without creating evil. This evil is not overcome in an earthly Jerusalem or in a new aeon. It is overcome only when we return to the no-thing-ness that is both our source and our end. The price we pay for existence is pain, suffering, anxiety, hopelessness, and evil. It is for this reason that I cannot accept Dr. Altizer's apocalyptic image. It seems too hopeful. It seems too quick a dance of joy at the great funeral.

Dr. Altizer has also spoken hopefully of America's vocation as being cut off from the past and oriented toward the future. I believe that few aspects of American life are as problematic as our lack of a sense of history. This has frightened Europeans as divergent in attitude as Albert Camus and Charles de Gaulle. They regard America as an adolescent nation precisely because of our lack of a sense of the past and the continuing inheritance of the dilemmas of the past in the present. In the long run, it is America's destiny to become Europeanized. What we are experiencing in Vietnam is a sense of limit, defeat, and the ironies of history. For several centuries we were able to separate ourselves geographically from the problems of European man. When we did not find things to our liking, we went farther west. That time is past. Eventually we will find that our situation is as tragic, as replete with evil as well as good, as the European situation has been throughout its entire history.

One of the things I like about the academic life is that it has given me an opportunity to spend some time in the Mediterranean in the summertime. There is swimming; there is beauty; there are joys of the flesh. All the joys Dr. Altizer believes are possible for Americans after the death of God are freely given in the Mediterranean landscape. But, as Albert Camus pointed out in "Summer in Algiers," what you buy with the flesh you pay for with death. The beauty of the Mediterranean is the beauty of Earth, the great mother goddess who gives birth to her children, allows them their moment in which to be fruitful and beautiful, in order that she may in her own time consume them. Earth, the great mother goddess, is a cannibal goddess. We have no reason to rejoice before her.

Dr. Altizer has a highly original interpretation of the meaning of Captain Ahab's quest for the great white whale in *Moby Dick*. According to Dr. Altizer, "Ahab's mad quest for the white whale can be seen as faith's response to the death of God, wherein the man of faith becomes the murderer of God so as to make possible a historical actualization of God's death in Jesus, and thus an apocalyptic consummation of God's original self-sacrifice or self-negation." Dr. Altizer sees Ahab as a paradigmatic figure. He seeks the death of God in order to bring about the apocalyptic liberation from the restraints of the dead God which is America's true mission. I agree with Dr. Altizer's high regard for *Moby Dick*. There is, however, one crucial speech of Captain Ahab's which Dr. Altizer seems to ignore. It is the speech at the very end in which the mad captain tells Starbuck of his forty years upon the sea. He declares that he did not marry until past fifty. His wife was not truly his wife, but a widow. He had hardly put a dent in the marital pillow before returning to sea. Having pursued his mad quest for forty years, he would not now desist from seeking the whale in spite of Starbuck's pleas.

Melville was not unfamiliar with Biblical imagery and symbolism. I do not believe that his use of Ahab's forty-year sojourn on the seas was accidental. The forty years on the sea represent Ahab's years in the wilderness. The great white whale is the Captain's Promised Land. As much as he hates the whale, as much as he wants to destroy the creature, he yearns unknowingly to be consumed by it. Erich Fromm has made a very interesting point about the story of Jonah and the whale: When Jonah is swallowed by the whale, he returns to the womb. God has charged Jonah to preach to the people of Nineveh. Jonah avoids his task. His ultimate withdrawal from adult responsibility is symbolized by his being consumed. The whale is the only creature large enough to enclose an adult man. The yearning to return to the source is a yearning to end the agonies and the problematics of the human condition. What troubles Captain Ahab is precisely the fact that we live in a malignant universe, in which human existence is filled with anxiety. As he says in one place, it is a cannibal universe underneath the calm, placid sea. There is only one way to escape. It is certainly not the New Jerusalem. *Moby Dick* does not end with the New Jerusalem. It ends with Ahab consumed by the whale, destined to be dissolved in the cannibal sea. Ahab returns to the nothingness out of which he has come. What Ahab fears and hates is that which he also yearns for. I hope that *Moby Dick* is not the paradigm of the new American, as Dr. Altizer suggests. There are Europeans who fear that it is. If *Moby Dick* is the paradigm of the new American, we will not have the tolerance for the ambiguity, the irony, the hopelessness, and the meaninglessness of the historic eras that dawn ahead of us. Lacking his tolerance, we will choose self-destruction rather than the pain of an incomplete and not entirely desirable existence.

Incidentally, not only does this imagery of arising out of nothing and returning to nothing make its appearance in the Kabbalism of Isaac Luria, and I suspect in Melville, but also in the psychoanalysis of Sigmund Freud in *Beyond the Pleasure Principle,* in which Freud sees life as a struggle between the desire to maintain individual identity and the desire to return to the source from whence we have come.

I wonder whether America can accept the death of God. I hope that it can. I understand that Dr. Altizer has been getting a lot of angry letters lately. Every American accepts the death of God in one sense. Dr. Altizer is right in characterizing our refusal to accept this event as "bad faith," *mauvaise foi,* as Sartre uses the phrase. The fact that Dr. Altizer and the other "death of God" theologians show the naked mirror of the self to America does not mean that America will thank them. Who knows what forms of secular tyranny and secular security America may choose rather than endure the awesome anxiety of a hopeless and meaningless cosmos? Dostoevsky saw this in the legend of the Grand Inquisitor. Men will choose bread, miracles, and security rather than the truth and freedom. The sad few who acknowledge the truth will not rejoice in it.

In conclusion let me add a warning. Two years ago I was invited to lecture at a German theological conference in Recklinghausen. One of the questions I was asked was, "What do you think about eschatology?" My answer was, "Eschatology is a sickness." I want to say to all of you as Christians—and this is a difficult thing to say—it was our Jewish sickness originally. We gave it to you. You took us seriously. Would that you hadn't! Would that you hadn't for your sakes and ours! But as a Jew who has known this sickness, let me warn you. Do not be tempted by it if you become post-Christian. If you are Christian, you cannot avoid it. If you become post-Christian, choose pagan hopelessness rather than the false illusion of apocalyptic hope.

One of the insights I find psychologically most completely on target in Christian theology is the old Augustinian-Calvinist notion of original sin. It is an anthropological insight that cannot be negated even in the time of the death of God. Perhaps especially *in* the time of the death of God, we must not lose sight of the fact that man does not cease to be a guilty or sinful creature. Original sin suggests an important impediment to apocalyptic enthusiasm at the death of God.

In conclusion I want to tell you of the way Isaac Bashevis Singer ends his novel, *The Family Moskat*. The Germans are before the gates of Warsaw in September, 1939. One of the brothers, realizing that Hitler is at the gates of Warsaw, affirms, as Jews have for thousands of years: "I believe in perfect faith that the Messiah will come speedily in our days." The other brother is astonished and says: "How can you say this?" The first replies: "Surely he will come. Death is the messiah." There is only one way out of the ironies and the ambiguities of the human condition: return to God's nothingness, the radical non-being of God and death.

THE AMBIGUITIES OF INNOCENCE

Charles H. Long

Mr. Altizer's first sentence refers to the image of America which now threatens to pass into the opposite of its original promise. I am not quite clear about what he means by *the* image of America. It seems to me that America has never been defined by any one image; rather, as a culture, it has always been in the process of becoming an image. The problem of what or who is an American has for this reason always evoked the most intense response from Americans.

However, in spite of this qualification, the question of the American image is one way of raising an important issue, for America from its very beginning has defined a hermeneutical situation—a situation in which *homo Americanus* was continually trying to discover and decipher the meaning of his being in the context of the most intense new and radical experience of Western man. It is the problem of understanding and identity that lies at the heart of America's problematic culture.

If the meaning of America constitutes a hermeneutical awareness, whatever deciphering is done must itself be rooted in the very problematic character of American culture. I can understand why William Blake's poem, *America*, attracted Mr. Altizer, for it is a poetic-mythological deciphering of America as a peculiar structure of human experience. I would rather follow another course in my deciphering, a course more modest and nonpoetic, but nevertheless, more akin to my hermeneutical talents.

F. D. Schleiermacher once remarked that every hermeneutic begins with or presupposes a misinterpretation—a statement with far-reaching implications for every hermeneutical task. Mr. Altizer shows an awareness of some of these implications when he speaks of the original promise of America which is now threatened. He continues his discussion of the misinterpretations of America through his analysis of Blake's *America* and Melville's *Moby Dick.* It is, however, necessary for us to know in a manner less impressionistic and poetical the nature of this misinterpretation, for it is the misinterpretations that constitute the problem of interpretation and it is by going through the misinterpretations that a new awareness of the problem will take shape. Any new interpretation will possess not only clarity but depth insofar as it struggles seriously with the misinterpretations. I am suggesting that if America now presents the possibility of a new interpretation of human reality, then we must at this moment in our history raise to an awareness the misinterpretations which have prompted this new hermeneutical situation.

From a religious point of view, the American experience expresses what Rudolf Otto described as *mysterium fascinosum.*[1] Otto describes by this term the quality of the religious object which attracts and evokes the desire for comfort, unification, and identification with the religious object. The contrasting attitude, *mysterium tremendum,* that quality which describes the distance of the object of religion from the worshiper, has been relegated to a residual category in the American experience. The deistic orientation of the founding fathers already presents us with a *deus otiosus,* a god who has removed himself from the center of this new world. His distance from the world of man does not inspire a sense of awe, majesty, or power, but indifference. The attention of the citizens of this new nation is focused on the more immediate realities which expressed themselves immanently in nature and human society. The statement of Benjamin Rush (one of Thomas Jefferson's scientific colleagues) of the connection between religion and nature is a case in point.

> The necessary and immutable connection between the texture of the human mind, and the worship of an object of some kind, has lately been demonstrated by the atheists of Europe, who, after rejecting the true God, have instituted the worship of nature, of fortune, and of human reason: and, in some instances, with ceremonies of the most expensive and splendid kind. Religions are friendly to animal life, in proportion as they elevate the understanding, and act upon the passions of hope and love. It will readily occur to you, that Christianity, when believed and obeyed, according to its original consistency with itself, and with the divine attributes, is more calculated to produce those effects than any other religion in the world. Such is the salutary operation of its doctrines and precepts upon no other argument, this alone would be sufficient to recommend it to our belief.[2]

It has been this direct relationship to the sacred, the *mysterium fascinosum*, the understanding of the sacred as immediately present through the forms of nature and the moral conscience, which constitutes a basic theme in the American experience.

This theme is so elemental in American experience that Perry Miller was able to interpret figures as dissimilar as Jonathan Edwards and Ralph Waldo Emerson as instances of the same religious sensibility. Miller states that

> the real differences between Edwards and Emerson, if they can be viewed as variants within their culture, lies not in the fact that Edwards was a Calvinist while Emerson rejected all systematic theologies, but in the quite other fact that Edwards went to nature, in all passionate love, convinced that man could receive from it impressions which he must then interpret, whereas Emerson went to Nature, no less in love with it, convinced that in man there is a spontaneous correlation with the received impressions. . . . Edwards sought the images or divine things in nature but could not trust his discoveries . . . but Emerson having

decided that man was unfallen announced no inherent
gap between mind and thing, that in reality they leap to
embrace each other.[3]

The important fact discerned here is the reliance on nature
as the mediator of the divine. It is this theme which has been de-
finitive for Americans. When it is stated that Americans have
no historical sense, the allusion is to this fact. It was that per-
ceptive observer of American culture, Alexis de Tocqueville, who
noted that "up to the present I don't see a trace of what we
generally consider faiths, such as customs, ancient traditions and
the power of memories."[4] The modality through which Americans
have experienced the ultimate has been that of nature rather
than history. "He who would understand America," says Sidney
Mead, "must understand that through all the formative years,
space has overshadowed time."[5]

If Americans have exploited their world, it has been an exploitation of nature; if they have suffered, it has been through
the forms of nature. It was precisely through theories of nature
that the destruction of the Indian cultures took place, and a
nation which at its inception proclaimed the equality of all men
was able to continue the institution of slavery under the guise
of nature. Allow me to continue this line of thought by presenting a rather long but almost lyrical quotation from Sidney
Mead:

> Americans during their formative years were a people in
> movement through space—a people exploring the obvious
> highways and the many unexplored by ways of practically
> unlimited geographical and social space. The quality of
> their minds and hearts and spirits was formed in that
> great crucible—*and in a short time.* Their great and obvi-
> ous achievement was the mastery of a vast, stubborn and
> oft-times brutal continent. This is the "epic of America"
> written with cosmic quill dipped in the blood, sweat and
> tears of innumerable little men and women. . . . This is
> the mighty saga of the outward acts, told and retold until
> it has overshadowed and suppressed the equally vital, but
> more somber story of the inner experience. *Americans*

*have so presented to view and celebrated the external and
material side of their pilgrim's progress that they have
tended to conceal even from themselves the inner experience, with its more subtle dimensions and profound
depths.*[6]

It is from this concealment that the innocence and naïveté
of the American emerges. The American has for one reason or
another never taken time to contemplate the ambiguity of act
and value, the horror and the evil which is synonymous with the
conquest of this new land. But this innocence of the American
is not a natural innocence, that innocence which is prior to
experience; rather, this innocence is gained only through an
intense suppression of the deeper and more subtle dimensions
of American experience. Americans never had or took the time
to contemplate the depth of their deeds. It is Mead again
who in a poignant manner speaks of this characteristic. He tells
of a cultivated New Englander who went to Oregon, and who
after shooting an antelope one day was given to this reflection,
"When I stood by his side, the antelope turned his expiring
eye upward. It was like a beautiful woman's, dark and bright.
Fortunate that I am in a hurry, thought I, I might be troubled
with remorse, *if I had time for it.*"[7]

Again in reference to Bernard de Voto's historical writing,
Mead sees the same theme. "Perhaps," says de Voto, "the
Indians might have been adapted to the nineteenth-century
order and might have saved enough roots from their own order
to grow in dignity and health in a changed world—*if there had
been time.*"[8]

If Americans are not conscious of history, it is not because
they are innocent. It is due to the fact that the depth of the
American experience lies in a relationship with nature as a
model of ultimate reality. The tendency of Americans to de-
emphasize history and the modality of time—the saga of the
mighty outward acts—represents a suppression, and the god of
American history results as an image of this suppression. In
having a god in this image Americans are able to repress the

profound and agonizing relationship which has defined their
being in space and nature. There may indeed be an authentic
god of time and history in the American experience, but such
a god is, in the words of James Weldon Johnson, "a God of our
weary years and a God of our silent tears."[9]

Now, this theme of innocence is not merely an intuitive or
impressionistic characterization of American culture; it has
played an important role in American historiography. A recently published work, David Noble's *Historians Against History*,[10] is based on the thesis that the major American historians
since 1830—Bancroft, Turner, Beard, Parrington, and Boorstin—
resist the very notion of history as a meaningful category for the
interpretation of American experience. Noble states that these
historians

> asserted that the reality of the American experience was
> the Puritan covenant translated into the material form of
> the Jeffersonian republic. Americans, they wrote, live not
> as members of a historical community with its inevitable
> structure of institutions and traditions, but as children of
> nature who are given earthly definition by the virgin land
> that had redeemed their ancestors when they stepped out
> of the shifting sands of European history.[11]

Noble exempts only Carl Becker from this judgment. Becker,
according to Noble, reluctantly gave up the naturalistic interpretation and sought a historical structure that would relate
the American experience to its roots in the past of Western
culture. Charles Sanford,[12] another American historian, notes the
same tendency when he analyzes the paradise myth in American culture. He concludes his work with the hope that Americans might in their contemporary experience learn to accept
and live with a tragic view of life.

Mr. Altizer puts his finger on this theme of innocence when,
in his paper, he discusses Melville's *Moby Dick*. Of Captain
Ahab, he says, "Ahab is at once an embodiment of the dark
altar of America—he has made the full transition from 'Inno-

cence' to 'Experience.' " Mr. Altizer's discussion of Ahab is accurate, vivid, and convincing. Ahab is willing to launch his ship into the deeper shark-infested waters of life—life beyond innocence.

Allow me at this point to clarify and summarize my reaction to this problem of innocence, nature, and history in American experience. Those historians referred to by Noble, from Bancroft to Boorstin, may have become convinced of the categories of the nature-history dichotomy as methodological principles by the content of the documents with which they dealt. In my opinion, and I tried to bring this out earlier in my citations from the work of Sidney Mead, Americans have in fact thought of themselves in this manner. However, like Noble, Sanford, and Altizer, I am convinced that innocence and nature are not enough and, I add, not a true rendering of American experience. Noble and Sanford leave us with only a hope that contemporary Americans will accept a tragic view of life, thus moving us beyond innocence. If I read Altizer's paper correctly, he presents to us the radical eschatological movement of a Captain Ahab. "As a tragic hero," Altizer says, "Ahab has no 'choice'; he must seek out and kill Moby Dick. . . . His tragic conflict with the white whale brings upon himself the death that he would inflict upon the whale, and by dying while lashed upon the whale's back he plunges into the sea of chaos and is swallowed up by the sepulcher of God."

Are our only choices for a movement beyond innocence to be defined by the vague hope of our historians and the eschatological and apocalyptic vision of Ahab? The hopes are too vague and, in my opinion, whatever is profound and true in the figure of Ahab is undercut by Ahab's inability to communicate and to be understood by his crew. His is the lonely and heroic stance of a Faustian man, and while he presents us with a vision of life on the far side of innocence, his vision is, in the last analysis, demonic, incommunicable, and escapist.

But more than this, I object to what I consider to be the call for an abrupt and radical movement beyond nature and innocence into history and experience. I object because such a movement fails to take account of the evil inflicted on nature during this so-called period of innocence. America in a certain sense has not been a virgin land since the establishment of the first colonies. To view American culture as if it has been some kind of Polynesia of Western culture is hermeneutically unsound because such a view fails to understand that through this modality of nature America was exploited through innocence and repression. Any movement to experience and history must in the end reconcile itself with nature, not in innocence, but in redemption. I am saying that America cannot affirm the future until it affirms its past. An eschatology that does not redeem the body of nature as well as announce a consummation to history can easily turn into just another ideology of power.

I discern hints as I follow Altizer's dialectic that he is concerned about this same issue, but one can never be sure with a dialectic, and especially with Altizer's.

There is finally another point to be raised here with Altizer. One might refer to it as the issue of tone or style—I am trying to speak of the mood evoked by the paper. In reading it, I caught a sense of great passion, urgency, radicality—and, I must add paradoxically, naïveté and innocence. On this level, which may ultimately be the most important, I felt that Altizer was portraying exactly the kind of innocence which he himself has set out to conquer. Like Mead's New Englander who killed an antelope but who is afraid to be confronted by the gaze of his great and beautiful dying eye, Altizer has not the time. He is a man who speaks of death glibly, as if he has never experienced or is afraid to experience the dying and the killing itself. He wishes for us to plunge on or—to put it in Frederick Jackson Turner's language—to move on to a new frontier. There is no patience, no meditative attitude, no attentiveness in his proposal.

The eschatological mythology which Altizer proposes is not rooted in that basic contact with reality which is the touchstone of every myth. It presents us with a rich exterior and a glorious future, but it has no interiority, no depth—a Gnostic dialectic substitutes for the depth of primary appearances of reality. What has been forgotten in all this talk about death is the humanity of death or, to put it another way, the religious meaning of death. It is a characteristic of human perception and imagination that any form of the world may signify meaning—even the dead continue to signify; if God is dead, the signification is even greater. Mr. Altizer, I suspect, has for this very reason not taken account of the fact that there might very well be another attitude in the American experience, an attitude that has confronted the reality of America, not as a plastic and flexible reality, amenable to the will of man through hard work and moral fortitude, but a reality impenetrable, definite, subtle, a reality so agonizing that it forced the American to give up his innocence while it at the same time sustained him as joy and promise. I am speaking of a quality of the American experience which through its harsh discipline destroyed forever the naïve innocence, simultaneously revealing a God of both nature and time—a God of our silent tears and a God of our weary years. This is indeed a tragic vision of life and nature. It is not unique to the Negro community in America, for it is present as a theme in American literature. It is a portrayal of the subtle and profound depths that lie at the heart of American culture.

Precisely at this time in American history, when we see our symbols, language, and behaviors in danger of being emptied of their meaning, we at the same time see the possibility of a renewal of our language, symbols, and behaviors. But can this task be accomplished by the exorcistic and heavy-handed style of the "death of God" rhetoric? Such a style is related to the power symbolism of an inauthentic god of repression, a god that Altizer ostensibly seeks to destroy. I propose a more modest orientation—one that might be able to affirm nature as a non-innocent reality and at the same time open up the possibility of a true historical future.

It may be true that America has the best possibility for setting the style for the future, but America must come to terms with its own depth in reality before it can move authentically into a future. It is not a coincidence that the basic problems which confront us as a nation today result from the fact that we have not taken the integrity of nature seriously. The exploitation of our natural resources and of Negroes and other racial minorities stem from this fact. Until we come to terms with these dimensions of our experiences and the meanings resulting from them, any future will be an escapism sustained only by the physical and psychological repression. America is the youngest of the nations of the West, but it is the oldest of the new democracies. Its future lies in its ability to live with, support, and understand the new world of Asia and Africa. While America is related in a special manner to Europe, European culture cannot become an absolute cultural norm for the American.

The challenge before America is not so much eschatological as it is reflective. Let us now take the time for this reflection on who we are.

NOTES

1. Rudolf Otto, *The Idea of the Holy*, 2d ed., tr. by John W. Harvey (London: Oxford University Press, 1950), Ch. VI.

2. Quoted by Daniel J. Boorstin in *The Lost World of Thomas Jefferson* (Beacon Press, Inc., 1960), p. 154.

3. Perry Miller, *Errand Into the Wilderness* (Harper Torchbooks, The Academy Library, 1964), p. 185.

4. Quoted by G. W. Pierson in *Tocqueville and Beaumont in America* (Oxford University Press, 1938), p. 153.

5. Sidney Mead, *The Lively Experiment* (Harper & Row Publishers, Inc., 1963), p. 11.

6. *Ibid.*, p. 8 (my italics).

7. *Ibid.*, p. 4 (my italics).

8. *Ibid.*, p. 5 (my italics).

9. This is a line from the pen of James Weldon Johnson, Negro poet and writer, quoted from his song "Lift Every Voice and Sing." This song was, until the middle of the 1950's, referred

to quite seriously in the Negro community as "The Negro National Anthem."

10. David Noble, *Historians Against History* (University of Minnesota Press, 1965).

11. *Ibid.*, p. 176.

12. Charles L. Sanford, *The Quest for Paradise* (University of Illinois Press, 1961).

II

THEOLOGY AND LANGUAGE

Jules Laurence Moreau

The confluence of two streams of intellectual development in the academically trained theologian of the twentieth century raises the question of whether we can use religious language meaningfully. On the one hand, the rise of scientific Biblical criticism which came of age in the last century and developed into responsible maturity in the early decades of the present century posed historical questions to systematic theology. The theological construct that owed its parentage to Ritschl and reached a sort of classical and popular expression in Adolf Harnack was *an* answer to those historical questions. The advent of a new phase of Biblical criticism which reflected a somewhat different approach to history and historical documents was at once a telling blow to the theological construct championed by the *Epigoni* of Harnack and the occasion for a new theological stance represented by such divergent figures as Barth, Tillich, Bonhoeffer, and Bultmann. This is one stream that flows into and through the contemporary academically trained theologian.

The other stream is philosophy, which has also undergone a transformation little short of revolutionary in the last three quarters of a century. The current philosophical concern with language, its meaning and function, has put Christian theology on the defensive in a singular way. Linguistic analysis has forced theologians to make sense within an empirically oriented world, but the sense that they claim to be making is not the same across the spectrum of modern expositions of Christianity. The number of books that have been published in the last few years dealing with the question of language and religion testifies to the presence of a real question which can be formulated somewhat as follows: Do religious statements have a meaning recognizable by people outside the religious community?

Apart from the succession of books which have been written chiefly by those Christian theologians whose primary interest has been in the philosophy of language, there is evident a much more theologically oriented concern. This can best be seen by a brief examination of what has been (somewhat erroneously, perhaps) called the "Cambridge Movement" in theology. The most responsible representative of this direction is the symposium *Soundings: Essays Concerning Christian Understanding.*[1] This collection of essays is a serious attempt to grapple with the simple fact that the traditional language of Christian theology fails to make any impact on the modern man whose entire conception of life is expressed in empirical terms. The effect of this symposium is still limited in its scope to the academic world. In part this is due to the relative abstruseness of some of the essays, but it is also due to the appearance of another more popular work stemming from the same general milieu which has captured the imagination of the general public and cannot help casting reflections upon the soberer theological effort of *Soundings.* The debate engendered by Dr. Robinson's *Honest to God* is indicative of the importance for academic theology of the questions raised by the results both of historical scholarship and of philosophical analysis. Hardly belonging in the same category as *Soundings,* this popular tract has drawn attention to the more serious work if only by the association of its author with the men who were responsible for the symposium. Another manifestation of the Cambridge Movement is the more recent tetralogy called *Objections to Christian Belief,*[2] edited by Alec Vidler, who was also responsible for assembling the essays in *Soundings.* As representative of one general outlook in attempting to deal with the question of meaning in religious assertion, these English essays show how deeply secular philosophical inquiry has penetrated theological thought.

The task that is set for theological inquiry is that of distinguishing what is peculiar to the Christian religious assertion from what is only incidental to communicating that assertion within a given cultural construct. Choice of the method by which that distinction is to be made depends in large measure upon the competence of the analyst who undertakes the task. This is certainly quite evident in the varied character of the essays that comprise *Soundings,* but it is all the more evident when we assemble the shelf of books that would properly come under the heading of "theology and language."

Paul van Buren, in his *The Secular Meaning of the Gospel,* suggests that the task of the interpreter of Christian language involves three concerns: preservation of the conservative interest in Christology, serious acknowledgment of the "liberal" intention to recognize contemporary thinking, and the acceptance of the logical analysis of religious and theological statements.[3] Such an approach to interpreting the language in which Christian believers commonly discuss would require not only a functional analysis of the entire corpus of the Biblical literature in order to ascertain what it means by what it is saying, but it would also require a functional analysis of the language of the growing body of theological reflection upon that literature which is represented by theological writing since the late first century. This undertaking would necessarily involve us in a synchronic study of each succeeding phase in the development of the history of Christian thought. While we do not propose that this is either the time or the place for such an analysis, we do insist that the scope of the task is at least this broad. Instead of the broad task, however, we should indicate the method involved and some application of it in paradigm cases.

In his now famous programmatic essay, Dr. Rudolf Bultmann set certain guidelines for dealing with the primary level of Christian language. His "Neues Testament und Mythologie"

proposed a radical reorientation of the method of New Testament interpretation practiced by his teachers.[4] Whereas the
liberal method of the nineteenth century was based upon a
critical approach whereby each successive story, discourse, or
logion was tested for authenticity, his method envisaged a slow
but responsible attempt to understand what each level of the
Gospel materials meant by the presentation of the materials
in a certain construct. Liberal criticism of the nineteenth century had as its goal the discovery of the historical Jesus; its
concomitant task was the interpretation of the picture of the
historical Jesus in contemporary terms. Everything that could
be assigned to the early church was to be discarded as destructive
of that picture of the historical Jesus. Bultmann's familiar statement from *The Theology of the New Testament* that the life and
preaching of Jesus were prolegomena to the theology of the
New Testament[5] was another way of drawing attention to the
fact that even in the basic literature of the Christian community
we are dealing not with mere reporting of bare occurrence but
with theological reflection upon experience. A fair assessment
of what he is trying to do will, however, reveal that he is
concerned with retaining the meaning of the New Testament
while making that meaning available to those for whom its
surface literal meaning is abhorrent.

I

This essay has grown from an emerging conviction that these
two efforts, one in theology and one in philosophy, are intimately
related, and that they are mutually supportive in showing the
direction toward evolving some acceptable criterion for meaning
in theological discourse. Because the phrase "theological discourse" may be rather ambiguous, it is probably best to begin
with an attempt at setting some boundaries to its meaning. In
this attempt at setting boundaries, we should take a cue from
Harmon Holcomb's critique[6] of an essay by Paul Holmer[7] in
which Holcomb tries to clarify Holmer's attempt to define the

sort of discourse that constitutes what has been designated by various writers as "the language of religion,"[8] religious language,[9] or theological language.[10] Holmer's essay drew a distinction between "language *about* religion" and the "language *of* religion," but did so in order more closely to define the language *of* religion. At some length Holmer points out that a good deal of the "systematic and principled study of religious materials . . . frequently passes as theology."[11] By the language *about* religion he meant such enterprises as sociology of religion, philosophy of religion, and other scientific disciplines that are analytic and descriptive in character instead of coming from the inside of the community. If the ambiguity to which we have referred is to be avoided, it is necessary to exclude from our present consideration this entire area of discourse, and to confine ourselves, rather, to what Holmer calls "the language of religious expression."[12] In order to avoid any further confusion, we should also wish to point out what Holcomb emphasizes when he says that strictly speaking it is improper to talk of "science, religion, etc., as having 'languages.' "[13] Because both "language *about*" and "language *of*" employ the vocabulary and the syntax of a common public language, we prefer to use the word "discourse" rather than "language," to indicate that the language employed to talk *about* religion has its own context and function distinct from that of ordinary language employed to give expression to religious affirmation. Each of these realms of discourse has a peculiar context and function for the common language employed in both.

It is this same distinction, that of context and function, which was made by Willem Zuurdeeg when he used the qualifier "convictional" to differentiate between the language of theological disciplines and that of their nontheological counterparts.[14] Some logical analysts may reject Dr. Zuurdeeg's use of the term "convictional" on the ground that it introduces a psychological dimension into what is primarily a logical problem; nevertheless, it is a most useful term, since it so well draws attention to the context and function of strictly theological discourse. The

similarity between the distinction being made by Zuurdeeg and
that by Holmer is underlined by an observation of Holmer who
says, "Theology is everywhere immured and permeated by an
overpowering religious passion."[15]

Within religious language, the realm of discourse that we have
tried to mark off from language about religion, there are a
number of different kinds of discourse which should be further
classified. Religious discourse comprises at least two levels of
discourse separable in analysis if not always in fact. The simplest
way to distinguish between these levels is to employ the differentiation used by Ferré, who means to separate the "language
of living faith" from the "language of academic theology"; the
former is peculiarly religious discourse, and the latter is systematic
discourse or simply theological discourse.[16] Even within the
realm of peculiarly religious discourse, different forms of utterance are distinguishable. Not all the statements which occur
within this broad context of religious discourse are assignable
to the same logical category. If we begin by assigning the
Biblical literature to the classification "religious language," it
becomes immediately evident on some closer scrutiny of the
kinds of statement to be found in this literature that much of
the narrative portion of such books as Samuel and Kings is of
the same logical order as any other historical statement. The
dates of accession for each of the Kings of Israel and Judah
are factual statements and can be classified as empirical statements. The statements that serve to make the chronicle a religious document, such as "He did what was evil in the sight
of the Lord" (I Kings 15:34), belong to the religious category,
for they presuppose a "living faith." Much of the material relating wars and other historical events belongs in the category
of empirical statements. When we come to those narratives
which report events that look like historical events, events
such as the Creation and the exodus, we realize that these are
not the same order of statement, even though grammatically
and otherwise they resemble an empirical statement. In these
statements, the element of miracle is present, but it is not present

in such a way that it can simply be "peeled off," producing an otherwise empirical statement. In both of these paradigm instances, the context is predominantly a religious one, and the locution is that of "living faith." On the whole, however, the Biblical literature is employed by the religious community to assert its living faith in the God who is the major actor in the story set forth. For that reason, we are justified in assigning the bulk of this material to the category of religious discourse, even if closer analysis could separate many statements out of the narrative as belonging to the class of empirical statements. What would be left would not have been remembered or retold except for the dimension of religious conviction which pervades the entire narrative of which these statements are a part. The categoreal mistake which is most frequently made in this regard is that of assigning the whole corpus of Biblical literature to the category of empirical statement. Recognition of the category of religious statement will not magically remove such categoreal mistakes, but it will provide the possibility of analyzing statements in the literature in order to keep the categories straight. This is one of the primary functions of historical research in the field of Biblical studies.

The recent discussions regarding the virgin birth and the resurrection are prime examples of categorial arguments. While the impetus for the analysis of the narratives which relate these purported events did not come in the first place from analytic philosophy, there is a certain rather close kinship between the historical scholarship which produced the critique of these narratives and the sort of analysis engaged in by linguistic philosophers. The method of a historian, such as Dr. Bultmann, who seeks to uncover the process by which the New Testament books achieved their completion and were ultimately collected into the canon of Scripture, is primarily analytic. The fundamental difference in approach between the form historians of this century and the liberal critics of last century is somewhat parallel to the difference in approach between the more recent practitioners of analytic philosophy and their precursors. Bult-

mann's program of *Entmythologisierung* began in an earnest
attempt to appreciate the kinds of utterance that are contained
in the New Testament. The classification of the various seg-
ments of the Gospels undertaken by form historians was a rudi-
mentary form of linguistic analysis. The search for the context
in which these basic forms were used and the attention paid to
that context proceeded from historical canons and criteria, but
the aim was quite similar to that of linguistic analysis. The conclusion that much of the material was employed in the context
of preaching in the early church served to emphasize that the
referent was somewhat different from that which the liberal
critics supposed. The result of this analysis which set the whole
body of the Gospel materials in a new light is succinctly contained in Dr. Bultmann's essay which set off the *Entmythologisierung* debate.[17] The enterprise of interpreting the New Testament proposed by Dr. Bultmann rests in the first instance upon
a detailed analysis of the materials that make it up.[18]

Bultmann's reliance upon existentialism as a vehicle for interpreting the New Testament may be contested on the ground
that the philosophical orientation he has chosen is inadequate
for the task. This objection does not necessarily imply that his
analysis is faulty; it may and indeed quite probably does indicate that he has emphasized one aspect of the New Testament
religious outlook to the near exclusion of another which is as
important. His basic contention that the New Testament "presents the event of Jesus Christ in mythical terms,"[19] is saying
from the standpoint of a historical critic something quite similar to what is being said from the standpoint of an analytic
philosopher such as Binkley who says that "religious language
. . . is an odd or extraordinary *use* of ordinary language."[20]

Within the classification of religious discourse, it would also
be appropriate to distinguish certain other types of utterance
that are directly dependent upon the language of the Bible.
First of all, we should point to the entire range of liturgical
language, the language of preaching, and the language of creedal
affirmations. During most of the history of the church, the

church's worship served as the context in which preaching based upon the creedal affirmations and ultimately upon the Bible took place. The early church used Scriptures primarily in the context of worship. As the liturgy developed, it patterned itself after the synagogal worship of the Jews, which was organized about the regular reading of the Law and the Prophets with an exposition of the particular reading that formed the lection of the day. As the Christian liturgy developed, it adapted this by replacing Torah reading with Gospel lection, and the exposition with a sermon based on that Gospel lection. The peculiarly Christian message was proclaimed in this context by authoritative interpreters of the events which were considered central by the church; these events in time became the framework of the *regulum fidei* and thus gave shape to the creeds. In this process there grew up in the church a tradition whereby what Bultmann calls the mythic presentation of the event of Jesus Christ was reiterated not only in proclamation but also in the liturgical performance that was the central act of the church's life. Since none but those who had been initiated could participate in the peculiar Christian worship, the catechumens who were being prepared for initiation were excluded from the central liturgical act of the community until they had learned all that was required of them and indicated their acceptance of the gospel by repeating the baptismal creed which was cast in this mythic form.

In essence, the creedal affirmation required of the baptizand was the basic summary of the faith upon which the New Testament rested. The similarity between what is known as the kerygma and the creedal affirmation required of these initiates is a further indication that the category "religious language" is apt for the creeds also. The fundamental difference between the language of the liturgy on the one hand and that of the creeds and the Scriptures on the other is one of address. Scriptures and creed are primarily narrative and in part propositional; the narrative is derived from the kerygmatic origin of the Bible and creed alike so that in this type of expression the reference to

God is in the third person. In the liturgy proper, the language is primarily vocative; even though it may preserve some of the narrative form of Scripture, the liturgical narrative is enfolded within the address—"O God who . . ." as compared with "We believe in the God who . . ." Scripture, liturgy, and creed are similar to the language of preaching as the historic church has understood this activity. From the earliest paradigm sermons in The Acts to the *Marburger Predigten* of Rudolf Bultmann,[21] the sermon of the Christian preacher has rooted itself in the language and images of the Bible and particularizes for the immediate congregation the proclamation that is contained within the total context of Scripture.

Not all the language of religious thought and expression is cast in the historical and narrative form. In fact, it would be fair to estimate that far more than half of what has been written through the ages of the Christian church has an entirely different framework. This is what we should call academic theology or systematic theology. One characterization of this facet of the entire religious enterprise is offered by G. C. Stead:

It is unilluminating to say that all religious language is theological. Theology is marked off, not so much by the kind of language used as by the use made of it.[22]

What Mr. Stead goes on to say is that systematic theology arises from the use of simple religious language in a deliberate attempt to correlate, support, and modify the expressions of "unreflective piety." Early attempts to argue the Christian affirmation at the bar of reason meant that the argument was carried on in the framework of systematic philosophy current in the Hellenistic world. Because the Christian intellectuals who began this enterprise were themselves participants in the world of philosophical discourse, the choice of a framework in which the discussion and correlation was carried on was already dictated. Not only were the theologians of the early church trained for the most part in the philosophical thought of middle and late Platonism, but they were also deeply involved in the understanding of their own religious affirmation. Hence, the theological enterprise that they prosecuted was as much an exercise in achieving intellectual integrity as it was an attempt to justify the Christian affirmation to nonbelievers. These two processes converged in the systematic theology which emerged in the course of the first few centuries of this era.

The argumentative character of systematic theology in the early centuries of the church's life is demonstrated during the conciliar period. Time after time, in settlement of theological arguments among those who sought to express their religious affirmation in philosophical terms, recourse was had to a formulary statement to which subscription was required. The alleged source for these formulary statements was in the language of living faith. The paradigm case of this method was that of the Council of Nicaea where a creedal affirmation cast in terms very similar to those of a baptismal creed was expanded by the addition of words such as *homoousion tō patri* which were not strictly "religious language." The origin of the terms that were added to the creedal affirmation was primarily to be found in the language of Greek philosophy, but the juxtaposition of these terms and the terms of simple religious affirmation set up a *norm* for the way in which the terms of the religious affirmation were to be related when one used the terms of current Greek philosophy to express that relation. That is to say, the statements adopted by the Councils were meant to be *tests* of the language of systematic theology. These statements provided the verification of theological discourse, but instead of being a publicly available corpus of experience, they pointed to the religious experience of a definable community. This characterization of theological discourse is readily recognizable as falling under that prescription offered by Augustine in his commentary on the Fourth Gospel:

> *Intellectus enim merces est fidei. Ergo noli quaerere intelligere ut credas, sec crede ut intelligas; quoniam nisi credideritis, non intelligetis. (In Ioan. Ev. XXIX.6.)*

This strain of thought persists in the history of systematic theology and is again expressed by Anselm of Canterbury, who puts it thus:

Rectus ordo exigit, ut profunda Christianae fidei credamus, priusquam ea praesumamus ratione discutere. (Cur deus homo I.2.)

That this is the function and the context of systematic theology is still witnessed by modern theologians of whom we may take two examples. Alan Richardson of the Church of England writes:

A dogma is an articulation of what the Church believes, and it is the task of the theologian to articulate what is implicit in the existence of the Church. Only those who possess existential knowledge of the Church's faith and life are in a position to articulate its true meaning.[23]

Karl Barth appears to define theology in precisely the same way when he says:

Over against and alongside of the Church's proclamation there must go a Church theology, especially dogmatics. Theology . . . is . . . the Church's concentrated anxiety and concern about her most intimate responsibility. . . . The Church's proclamation . . . is at least also man's language about God. . . . Starting from the question how men spoke about God in the Church yesterday, dogmatics asks how this should be done tomorrow.[24]

What has been described by a succession of Christian thinkers from Augustine to Barth and practiced by a succession that reaches farther back and continues beyond them is what we should describe as theological language distinguishable from but springing out of the simpler language of living faith.

Elsewhere I have drawn the distinction between religious and theological language in slightly different terms but with similar intention. There I suggested that the language of academic theology stands midway between the scientific description of natural phenomena and a religious orientation to the world.[25]

To allow the distinction to rest there, however, is to permit the inference that theological language is static. This is far from the case, because even if the language of religious affirmation remains fixed (a dubious condition), the description of natural phenomena does not "stay put." Consequently, there is a real danger to religious language if the theological language of some era is treated as absolute; this is especially true if theological language is repeated without appreciating the context out of which it arose.

Religious language is thus not propositional if its religious context is understood; the Biblical exegete assures the Christian community constantly of the peculiar nature of religious language, while the historian of Christian thought keeps before the religious community the fact that its theological language is an attempt to relate the religious affirmation to the changing context in which the world of nature is appreciated. What kinds of tests are to be employed in placing religious and theological language in their proper relation to all other kinds of utterance is a question that has become singularly important in the recent past because of the advent of a philosophical orientation whose primary concern was with the function and meaning of language.

II

When verificational analysis applied its analytic tools to the language of systematic theology, its first judgment was that this language was not cognitive. Propositions such as "God exists" were ruled nonsensical because there were no sense data that would verify such a statement. The brief but devastating analysis of this statement, "God exists," by A. J. Ayer in his manifesto of 1936 is now a classic.[26] Since this brash book of his youth, Ayer has somewhat modified the harsher aspects of his thesis, but his main contention remains practically untouched: assertions about God are not cognitive. The chief criticism against this thesis is that the term "cognitive" is too narrowly conceived. In an essay on this subject, Frederick Ferré deals directly with this point and offers some way out of the impasse that results from doctrinaire assertions made on each side of the argument.[27] The context of Ferré's discussion requires some delineation, however, before the chief value of these suggestions can be assessed.

Linguistic analysis, in its early stages as represented by Ayer and his contemporaries, divided all statements into three general classes according to the way in which they could be verified: analytic, synthetic, and emotive. Because emotive statements could not be verified, it was the contention of this school of thought that the only proper function of language lay in the making of analytic and synthetic statements; all others were meaningless in that they could not be verified or falsified.[28] According to this viewpoint, analytic statements as distinguished from synthetic statements depend solely for their validity upon the definitions of the symbols they contain. Ayer's instance of a system composed entirely of analytic statements is a geometry, about which he says, "All that the geometry itself tells us is that if anything can be brought under the definitions, it will satisfy the theorems."[29] This is to say, a geometry is not a study of the physical properties of space but is a closed system depending upon definitions, axioms, and postulates; all the conclusions are inherent in the half dozen a priori assumptions upon which the geometry is based. On the other hand, synthetic statements depend for their validity upon the facts of experience. All other statements fall in the general class of emotive statements. The only cognitive statements are synthetic statements, and the basis of their being cognitive is that they may be verified by recourse to sense data. Analytic statements, though not cognitive, are important because they supply the "rules of the road" for the use of language. Analytic statements and synthetic statements together make up all the significant discourse because their meaning can be determined. All other statements, being exempt from the verification process, may be true or false, but there is no way of showing them to be either.

The value of this distinction cannot be denied, for it does help to sort out many statements which may appear grammatically alike but which are in fact not similar logically. A simple example of this sort of analysis is afforded when we ask what the statement "God created the world" means. This looks very much like the statement "The cat ate the fish," for both consist of a subject, a transitive verb, and an object. The latter does give information, says the logical analyst; it is cognitive, because it is open to verification by reference to specific experience. What would count as verification or conversely as falsification of this statement is accessible. The important distinction between the two statements is not whether or not one actually does verify them but whether one or the other *can* be verified.

As a theological statement, "God created the world" cannot be verified; therefore, despite its grammatical similarity to the other statement, it must be of a different order. What sort of statement is it? It may be an analytic statement. Thus conceived, the statement is meant not to convey some information about a fact of experience but to tell how the word "God" is used. If this statement is only an analytic statement, it is an a priori and cannot give us any more information than is contained in the assumption upon which it rests.

The other possibility, that theological language is emotive, is the result of an analysis such as that made by R. B. Braithwaite whose conclusion is that "the primary element in this use [of language] is that the religious assertion is used as a moral assertion."[30] Instead of using the more familiar term "emotive" to characterize this language, however, Braithwaite dulls the pain caused the theist by calling it "conative" and thus allows what many Christians would contend anyway: that theological language arises from the worship of the Christian community and shapes its behavior. Behind the conative meaning of theological language, some logical analysts would call attention further to a body of supporting material.

Hepburn, who follows Braithwaite but carries his analysis farther, calls this "parable,"[31] but he does not insist upon the truth of the parable. Hepburn thus sees that the body of credenda is important for Christian language, even if he does not think that it is of primary importance. An ample criticism of this evaluation of theological language as primarily emotive or ethical (conative) is made by R. M. Hare who insists that the real problem in all theological language still rests in the area of what is believed and its relation to fact.[32] While he does accentuate the necessity of some attitude toward the world as logically *prior* to knowing any facts, his contention that the facts which are relevant to a person with a religious attitude are not other than ordinary facts[33] seems to have the religious men say what even Ayer said was not what the religious man meant when he made religious statements. Despite its salutary (for theologians) insistence upon the central importance of religious attitude for the ordering and understanding of life, Hare's analysis of theological language seems to reduce such language to statements about the natural world. As Ayer pointed out:

> It is often claimed, indeed, that the existence of a certain sort of regularity in nature constitutes sufficient evidence for the existence of a god. But if the sentence "God exists" entails no more than that certain types of phenomena occur in certain sequences, then to assert the existence of a god will be simply equivalent to asserting that there is the requisite regularity in nature, and no religious man would admit that this was all he intended to assert in asserting the existence of a god.[34]

Consequently, while they grant considerable meaning to theological discourse instead of merely consigning it to the category of non-sense, Braithwaite, Hepburn, and Hare cannot bring theological language out of the "emotive" closet where Ayer and his contemporaries have put it. It is quite possible that this is where it belongs, and that if we are to do anything about making sense out of theological discourse, we shall have to accept this classification.

One way to deal with the critique of philosophical analysis is to admit that its contentions are correct and to proceed from there by pointing to the unique function of theological discourse while really avoiding the question of the truth or falsity (i.e., the verifiability) of sentences in this kind of discourse. As a sample of this approach we can cite Binkley's essay in which he distinguishes seven classes of statement found in this kind of language.[35] After pointing out that there are some empirical (i.e., synthetic) statements made in religious contexts—e.g., factual statements about Jesus' birth, crucifixion under Pontius Pilate, etc.,—and that there are some patently tautological (i.e., analytical) statements in this discourse—definitional statements about God and Jesus Christ that imply nothing about existence or fact— he goes on to enumerate five other classes of statement: emotive, performative, prescriptive, mythical, and paradoxical. In his comments on this article, John Hick accuses Binkley of leaving out of his analysis of this language the most important class of statement, i.e., that which makes a statement of religious fact, which Hick would call metaphysical.[36] Binkley's reply is that statements such as Hick offers—e.g., "God loves mankind"—do not actually assert fact because they are not verifiable.[37] In other words, while he has broadened the notion of noncognitive language so that it includes five subclasses, Binkley is consistent in accepting the dichotomy between cognitive and noncognitive statements. Like Ian T. Ramsey,[38] Binkley considers that the real function of theological discourse in its manifold forms is to achieve discernment-commitment rather than to disclose facts. Consequently, it appears that Binkley and Ramsey are but a short distance removed from Alasdair MacIntyre, who says in almost so many words that one believes in the stories about God which make up the core of Christian belief *on authority*, "and this means, if you like, that religion as a whole lacks any justification."[39] By referring to religious discourse as one among several areas of thought and inquiry which "is defined by reference to certain ultimate criteria," he has come quite close to the notion of language games which would insist upon the autonomy of fields of thought and expression.[40]

If MacIntyre is right, then there does not seem to be any way out of the impasse. Theological discourse is not cognitive, at least in the sense of the term agreed upon by linguistic philosophy, and the only ground upon which the religious attitude-belief is adopted is one of authority. The problem which this assertion raises is stated well by Ernest Gellner, a sharp critic of linguistic philosophy whose training was in the technique of analysis. He contends, in speaking about religion and linguistic philosophy, that the argument "meaning is use . . . proves the validity not of any one religion, but of all of them, and [proves the validity also] of all denials of any one of them." In fact, he continues, "from the viewpoint of such philosophy it is impossible to evaluate or take sides in conflicts."[41] Gellner's answer to the difficulty is to get rid of linguistic philosophy, but there may be another less drastic way open. That would be to try to preserve the advances made by linguistic philosophy while trying to work out some useful criteria for ascertaining the truth of theological expressions.

III

The question that is posed for theological discourse by linguistic analysis is still a valid one: Are religious statements cognitive? If they are cognitive, it must further be asked whether there is any way of verifying or falsifying them. One way out of this problem is to expand the horizon of meaning in the word "cognitive" so that it will apply to more than empirically verifiable knowledge. The road to a broader understanding of the term "cognitive" as applied to religious or theological assertions seems to lie in a direction at least parallel to that suggested by Whitehead in connection with speculative philosophy. In defining speculative philosophy and defending it "as a method productive of important knowledge," Whitehead calls it "the endeavour to frame a coherent, logical, necessary system of general ideas in terms of which every element of our experience can be interpreted."[42] The use of ordinary language within theological contexts performs such a task, which is to say that such assertions are meant to express an orientation to the world in which all experience is comprehensible. If an advantage has been gained, even momentarily, by the expansion of the term "cognitive," we still have to face the question of the truth content of such assertions. This inevitably brings us back to the matter of verification. We may claim legitimately that the meaning of a theological or religious statement is not to be discovered by literal interpretation of the words employed, but we must yet show *how* this meaning is to be achieved. It is also incumbent upon us to demonstrate why one construct of such statements is preferable to another. That is to say, we must develop some criteria for determining the validity of one construct of theological assertions over another, or a method of distinguishing between real or claimed perception and mere hallucination.

Determining the validity of one such construct over against another involves two separate but related questions: (a) How do we acquire the categories within which we organize all aspects of our experience? and (b) Which categories of those possible ought we to choose? The answer to the former query involves a complete description of how men have derived the symbols about which they organize their total orientation to the world in which they find themselves. As a phenomenological inquiry this amounts to nothing less than an understanding of man's total quest for meaning of the world, himself, and his place in that world. An indispensable part of this quest for meaning is the history of man's religious enterprise. The answer to the latter question requires the development of canons of verification to determine the validity or invalidity of key religious experiences, expressed symbolically, around which an understanding of all experience is organized.

A religious affirmation, as a construct of related assertions, lays claim to being a coherent and adequate system of ideas by which all experience can be interpreted and understood. Any particular assertion within that construct has meaning only within the total construct. Thus the historical and descriptive aspects of the analysis of such a system will show *what* is meant by individual and particular assertions within the construct. This is tantamount to recognizing that ordinary language "counters" follow certain rules when they are used in the "language game" of scientific discourse, but these "counters" follow another equally valid set of rules when they are used in the language game of theological discourse. The language game of theological discourse may thus be coherent, but it is still to be determined whether it can stand the test of adequacy. Here is where the question of verification becomes relevant; if this use of language tells us anything about the world, we should be able to relate this language game to truth.

The verification of religious assertions cannot proceed in the same way as the verification of scientific assertions. Yet a valid set of criteria is demanded. As a means of advancing in this direction, three criteria for verifying religious assertions are suggested: aptness, adequacy, and efficacy.[43] These criteria are the result of reflection upon the previously cited definition of speculative philosophy offered by Whitehead. On the rational side, his definition contends for coherence and logicality but on the empirical side for applicability and adequacy. The two sides of this definition are united by an explanation of adequacy:

> The adequacy of the scheme over every item does not mean adequacy over such items as happen to have been considered. It means that the texture of observed experience, as illustrating the philosophic scheme, is such that all related experience must exhibit the same texture.[44]

The three criteria here suggested lie on the empirical side of Whitehead's definition, and thus they may be employed as canons of verification.

The religious outlook expressed in the Bible and developed in the theological language of the church is couched in images intended to do precisely what Whitehead defines as the function of speculative philosophy. Unlike the more or less traditional Western philosophical enterprise, it has taken its primary images from history rather than from nature. The first question to be asked of these images is whether they are suitable for what they are intended to do. Some symbols and images are more suitable for the task of providing an orientation to experience than others. The continued use of such images testifies to their historical aptness if not to their contemporary suitability. The first step in verifying religious assertions employing these images is to test their aptness.

Even if the aptness of the symbolic statements is demonstrated by test, even if their applicability is shown, there is the further test of whether they are adequate to account for and interpret all experience. This is the application of the canon of adequacy. If there is any part of experience which cannot be made comprehensible by these images, then they must fail the test of adequacy.

Moreover, there is a test which would go beyond those implied in Whitehead's definition of speculative philosophy. This test would ask what is the effect of the adoption of the total orientation inherent in a particular complex of religious assertions. Granted, there is demanded here an evaluation of effects, but surely an axiology is implied in any system that expresses total orientation to the world of experience.

If indeed religious language is cognitive, it must have certain criteria by which that quality can be tested. While these suggested criteria are only tentative, they are an attempt to show what function is performed by religious language and theological assertions, as well as to suggest some means of discrimination among rival religious systems on the basis of an appeal to a wider concept of truth.

NOTES

1. Alexander R. Vidler, ed., *Soundings: Essays Concerning Christian Understanding* (Cambridge: Cambridge University Press, 1962).

2. Alexander R. Vidler, *Objections to Christian Belief* (London: Constable & Co., Ltd., 1963).

3. Paul van Buren, *The Secular Meaning of the Gospel: Based on an Analysis of Its Language* (The Macmillan Company, 1963), p. 18.

4. Translated by Reginald H. Fuller in Hans Werner Bartsch, ed., *Kerygma and Myth: A Theological Debate* (Harper Torchbooks, The Cloister Library, 1961), pp. 1–44.

5. Rudolf Bultmann, *The Theology of the New Testament,* 2 vols. (Charles Scribner's Sons, 1951 and 1955), Vol. I, p. 3.

6. Harmon Holcomb, "Comment," *Journal for the Scientific Study of Religion,* Vol. I (1961–1962), pp. 55–60.

7. Paul L. Holmer, "Scientific Language and the Language of Religion," *Journal for the Scientific Study of Religion,* Vol. I (1961–1962), pp. 42–55.

8. *Ibid.,* p. 42 and *passim.*

9. L. J. Binkley, "What Characterizes Religious Language?" *Journal for the Scientific Study of Religion,* Vol. II (1962–1963), pp. 18–24.

10. Frederick Ferré, *Language, Logic, and God* (Harper & Brothers, 1961), p. vii.

11. Holmer, *loc. cit.,* p. 44.

12. *Ibid.,* p. 45.

13. Holcomb, *loc. cit.,* p. 58.

14. Willem F. Zuurdeeg, *An Analytical Philosophy of Religion* (Abingdon Press, 1958), p. 314 *et al.*

15. Holmer, *loc. cit.,* p. 46.

16. Ferré, *op. cit.*, p. viii.

17. See above, Note 4.

18. Rudolf Bultmann, *The History of the Synoptic Tradition,* tr. by John Marsh (Harper & Row, Publishers, Inc., 1963); *Das Evangelium des Johannes* (12th ed.; Göttingen: Vandenhoeck and Ruprecht, 1952); *The Theology of the New Testament.*

19. Bultmann, *Kerygma and Myth,* p. 34.

20. Binkley, "What Characterizes Religious Language?", *loc. cit.*, p. 21 (italics mine).

21. Rudolf Bultmann, *This World and the Beyond: Margburg Sermons,* tr. by Harold Knight (Charles Scribner's Sons, 1960).

22. G. C. Stead, "How Theologians Reason," in *Faith and Logic: Oxford Essays in Philosophical Theology,* ed. by Basil G. Mitchell (London: George Allen & Unwin, Ltd., 1957), p. 110.

23. Alan Richardson, *Christian Apologetics* (London: SCM Press, Ltd., 1947), p. 62.

24. Karl Barth, *Church Dogmatics,* Vol. I, *The Doctrine of the Word of God,* (Edinburgh: T. & T. Clark, 1936), Part I, pp. 84–86.

25. Jules Laurence Moreau, *Language and Religious Language: A Study in the Dynamics of Translation* (The Westminster Press, 1961), pp. 103 ff.

26. A. J. Ayer, *Language, Truth, and Logic* (rev. ed., Dover Publications, Inc., 1953), pp. 114–120.

27. Frederick Ferré, "Is Language About God Fraudulent?" *Scottish Journal of Theology,* Vol. XII (1959), pp. 337–360.

28. Cf. the summary of this viewpoint in Ferré, *op. cit.*, pp. 9 ff.

29. Ayer, *op. cit.*, p. 83.

30. R. B. Braithwaite, *An Empiricist's View of the Nature of Religious Belief* (Cambridge: Cambridge University Press, 1955), p. 11.

31. R. W. Hepburn, *Christianity and Paradox: Critical Studies in Twentieth-Century Theology* (London: C. A. Watts & Co., Ltd., 1958), p. 195.

32. R. M. Hare, "Religion and Morals," in Mitchell, ed., *op. cit.*, pp. 176–193.

33. *Ibid.*, pp. 189 f.

34. Ayer, *op. cit.*, p. 115.

35. Binkley, "What Characterizes Religious Language?", *loc. cit.*, pp. 18–22.

36. John Hick, "Comment," *Journal for the Scientific Study of Religion*, Vol. II (1962–1963), pp. 22–24.

37. L. J. Binkley, "Reply to Professor Hick's Comment," *Journal for the Scientific Study of Religion*, Vol. II (1962–1963), pp. 228–230.

38. Ian T. Ramsey, *Religious Language: An Empirical Placing of Theological Phrases* (London: SCM Press, Ltd., 1957), pp. 11–48.

39. Alasdair C. MacIntyre, "The Logical Status of Religious Belief," *Metaphysical Beliefs: Three Essays* (London: SCM Press, Ltd., 1957), p. 202.

40. L. Wittgenstein, *Philosophical Investigations* (The Macmillan Company, 1953), pp. 2–6, and intermittently throughout Part I.

41. Ernest A. Gellner, *Words and Things: A Critical Account of Linguistic Philosophy and a Study in Ideology* (London: Victor Gollancz, Ltd., 1959), pp. 221 f.

42. Alfred North Whitehead, *Process and Reality: An Essay on Cosmology* (The Macmillan Company, 1929), p. 4.

43. A not dissimilar series of canons is offered by Frederick Ferré in "Is Language About God Fraudulent?" *loc. cit.*, esp. pp. 357 f.

44. Whitehead, *Process and Reality*, p. 5.

II A

THE LANGUAGE GAME OF THEOLOGY

Joseph A. Johnson, Jr.

The basic problem with which we have been confronted by
Dr. Moreau is "whether we can use religious language meaningfully." This problem or question is forced on us by the rise
of scientific Biblical criticism, and by the development of linguistic analysis, which according to Professor Moreau ["has forced
theologians to make sense within an empirically oriented world."
"Do religious statements have a meaning recognizable by people
outside the religious community?" is the basic question with
which theologians are confronted today, according to Moreau.

Professor Moreau traces the rise of this movement, which he
calls "the philosophy of language," and indicates the task set
for theological inquiry: "that of distinguishing what is peculiar
to the Christian religious assertion from what is only incidental
to communicating that assertion within a given cultural construct."

Moreau presents his own analysis of the religious discourse
found in Scripture and in the Christian tradition, suggesting
the different types of discourse, underscoring the presence of
liturgical language, the language of preaching, and the language
of creedal affirmation. He reminds us that Biblical literature is
employed by the religious community to assert its living faith
in the God who is the major actor in the story set forth. Too,
we are reminded that "not all the language of religious thought
and expression is cast in the historical and narrative form. In
fact, it would be fair to estimate that far more than half of what

has been written through the ages of the Christian church has an entirely different framework. This is what we should call academic theology or systematic theology." Systematic theology arises from the use of simple religious language in a deliberate attempt to correlate, support, and modify the expressions of unreflective piety. The theological enterprise is concerned with achieving intellectual integrity on the one hand, and is an attempt to justify the Christian affirmation to nonbelievers.

Thus far in our comment on Professor Moreau's paper we have presented a summary of his interpretation and analysis. As a layman in this field, I wish to express my deep appreciation of his many profound observations, and the brilliant insights offered.

However, I wish to disagree with Professor Moreau when he submits systematic theology without reserve to the analytic tools of verificational analysis. When Professor Moreau advises us that "one way to deal with the critique of philosophical analysis is to admit that its contentions are correct and to proceed from there by pointing to the unique function of theological discourse while really avoiding the question of the truth or falsity of sentences in this kind of discourse," I must register a major disagreement. Though he attempts to move beyond this position, it is not clear that he succeeds. To be sure, I am aware of Moreau's effort to preserve the cognitive element of theological assertions by expanding the meaning of the term "cognitive" so that it will apply to more than empirically verifiable knowledge. Taking his lead from Whitehead, who defined speculative philosophy as "the endeavour to frame a coherent, logical, necessary system of general ideas in terms of which every element of our experience can be interpreted," he concludes that theological assertions are meant to express an orientation to the world in which all experience is comprehensible. Even within this context, theological assertions must be validated. Moreau defines a religious affirmation as "a construct of related assertions [which] lays claim to being a coherent and adequate system of ideas by which all experience can be interpreted and understood." He suggests that the three criteria for verifying religious assertions are: aptness, adequacy, and efficacy. This is promising, but it is a question whether it is sufficient.

I return to my major objection to Moreau's paper, namely, I do not admit that the critique of philosophical linguistic analysis and its contentions are correct, because even as this analysis is presented by Dr. Moreau, it comes perilously close to admitting that all theological statements are emotive.

Early linguistic analysis divided all statements into three general classes according to the way in which they could be verified. Analytic statements depend solely for their validity upon the definitions of the symbols they contain. Analytic statements are those which are true by necessity; they cannot be false. They do not tell us about empirical existence, and they are neither confirmable nor falsifiable by empirical investigation. The predicates of such statements only make explicit what was already contained in the subject. Synthetic statements depend for their validity upon the facts of experience. Their truth or falsity can be decided only by examining the empirical world. According to the verification principle, we must exclude from any claim to truth all synthetic propositions which cannot, at any rate in principle, be verified by sense experience—by what is seen, heard, touched, tasted, and smelled.

Emotive statements are those statements which are exempt from the verification process. Theological language, in this view, is emotive. According to Moreau, "Braithwaite, Hepburn, and Hare cannot bring theological language out of the 'emotive' closet where Ayer and his contemporaries have put it. It is quite possible that this is where it belongs, and that if we are to do anything about making sense out of theological discourse, *we shall have to accept this classification*" (italics mine).

It is interesting to note that whereas the linguistic analyst makes a very detailed and careful analysis of analytic and synthetic statements, he has a strange blindness to the significance of other statements. Instead of analyzing them, he tosses them into the wastebasket of "emotive language." This means that ethical, aesthetic, and theological language are thrown indis-criminately into a heap. Instead of developing a type of analysis appropriate to these many propositions, the linguistic analyst describes them in strangely emotional terms. Words with de-sirable connotations, such as "meaningful," "factual," "cognitive," and "sensible," are reserved for the language of science and logic. On the other hand, words that have pejorative connota-tions, such as "meaningless," "nonsensical," and "emotive," are applied to all other uses of language.

There is a need today to investigate the nature of *personal language*. In our day we have been conditioned to suppose that scientific knowledge is the perfect model for all forms of knowledge. In science, we tend to believe, there is the closest thing to certainty that man can have, because here the great conquests in the realm of knowledge have been made. Linguistic analysis is a philosophical expression of a mood that is wide-spread in our time. This mood assumes that if anything is not scientific knowledge, it cannot be knowledge at all. This is the hidden premise in most attacks on theological language that still come from analytical philosophers. Consequently, theology has been tempted to formulate its beliefs in terms of an analogy with the findings of science. But to do so is to assume, however subtly, that God is to be thought about as a thing. Furthermore, it is to overlook the fact that although science has been dra-matic in its results, there has always been another form of knowledge that is crucial for life—the knowledge of persons.

Professor Moreau referred to Zuurdeeg's understanding of religious language as "convictional" so as to differentiate be-tween the language of theology and the nontheological counter-parts.[1] The key to Zuurdeeg's position is to be found in a use that he makes of the concept "convictional language." He used the terms "conviction," "convictor," and "convicted." The word "conviction" means "to overcome, to conquer, to refute." The word "convictional" is used to bring out the fact that the man who speaks of his God, or of right or wrong, is not describing how he feels, but rather he is pointing to something which has "convicted" him. Therefore, the term is used by Zuurdeeg to cover all persuasions concerning the meaning of life, all value judgment, and all ideals. He contends that convictions are grounds for action. It is from convictions that decisions are made and life is governed. Convictional certitude moves the whole of life. The convictor is that which has the power to overwhelm and overawe. The convictor is presented through the "witness" of those who have been convicted, and to the convictor, so presented, man makes his response. When a man is convicted, he undergoes a radical change in the whole of his life. He has been "converted"; he is a new man. In a real sense a man is what he says in convictional language. Even though analytical philosophy claims to study language alone, one must remember that language is never an entity in itself. To study language, one must study the man who speaks. Therefore, man speaks convictional language to establish his existence, to find out who he is. To understand such language it is not sufficient to analyze its logical structure; we must identify who said it, in what circumstances, and what the man was trying to say with the language.

Convictional language is as much concerned to point to reality as is empirical language. Whether the reality referred to exists or not is not a question that analytical philosophy could decide in view of its own concepts of philosophy. Convictional language aims to deal with the whole of reality, whereas science confesses to deal with only certain relations between certain kinds of facts, that is, with a part of reality.

No language can be free from convictions. The scientist who extols objectivity is a man who has been convicted that impartial science is necessary for the good life. When the logical positivist claims that statements lacking logical or empirical verification are meaningless, he is expressing his conviction. When the atheist asserts that there is no God, he is expressing a conviction. When the Christian states that "God is," this, too, is a conviction. When the leaders of the "new theology" assert that "God is dead," that is their conviction.

Now what is the relation of convictional language to knowledge? That is, can convictional language be validated? In answering this question two quotations are in order: J. J. C. Smart declared, "In my opinion religion can stand on its own feet."[2] Smart is insisting that religion has within itself the ability to persuade. Theology has its own language game. Now, if theology has its own language game, what you can persuade any man to believe through the use of reason will be limited by the convictional framework the man holds. Use may be made of linguistic analysis in that it will enable one to detect the convictions, often hidden, in any analysis of theological language. This approach will not attempt to argue within the framework of a convictional pattern alien to Christian convictions.

William Blackstone's discussion of religious knowledge is suggestive in this connection.[3] He reminds us that there are many uses of the word "know." He argues that in order to judge whether a statement constitutes knowledge we must appeal to criteria that function as a norm for knowledge. The criteria that constitute a norm cannot "be confirmed as either true or false as can statements which conform to these criteria."[4] Now, what are the norms used in arriving at "justified knowledge claims"? Blackstone contends that justified knowledge claims must meet those requirements established by the canons of inductive and deductive logic. When one makes use of these methods and finds that his beliefs are supported by the data collected and interpreted by these "reliable methods," he is justified in claiming his beliefs to be knowledge. The "sound reasons" he gives for accepting these criteria and norms are the "pragmatic ones" that have been proved useful in practice. The ultimate and final test for theological and other assertions is not necessarily logic, though logic is included. The ultimate test is life.

We have already inferred that theology has its own language game, and we now add that theology cannot allow philosophy to prescribe the nature of its language game, any more than science has allowed philosophy to dictate the nature of its language game. Describing the nature of theological language is a theological task.

Let us consider how one particular language game may be distinguished from other language games.

First, use is a major means of distinguishing language games. For example, empirical language is used to refer to physical objects and their interrelationships. Ethical language is used to express what ought to be and to pass judgment upon acts. Secondly, language games are distinguished by different vocabularies. Thirdly, words in a language game are closely interrelated and may be definable only in terms of one another. Fourthly, language games can be distinguished by differing methods of verification. Finally, language games are rooted in different "convictional foundations."

When we assert that theological language forms a particular language game, we are inferring that it displays uniqueness in at least three features: (1) It has a particular use that is related to man's religious life. (2) It has its own vocabulary containing words that are ultimately definable within terms of one another, such as "God," "worship," "grace," and "sin." (3) It has its own means of verification based upon its own convictional basis.

Now, it has been argued that if theology is a separate language game, it is impossible to communicate with the unbeliever. Since it is impossible to translate terms from one game into another without distorting or losing their meaning, there is no logical way to communicate a language game to a man who does not already play the game. It is well to remember that it is logically impossible to argue a man into the Kingdom of God. There is a danger that the theologian who sees this will conclude that there is no way for the Christian to communicate with the non-Christian. However, we must remember that men do learn to use new language games. How is this possible?

Wittgenstein reminds us that to describe a different language game is to describe a different way of life. He also demonstrates that it is life, not philosophy, that teaches us new language games. In the light of this, we can see that Christian communication is never purely a matter of logic. The Christian must share with the unbeliever the way of life from which theological language comes. Then and only then can he hope to make his language game meaningful. It is impossible to persuade a man by logic that he ought not to steal if he has no sense of obligation or duty. Since terms like "ought" and "duty" are not translatable into nonethical terms, the man who has no experience of obligation in his life cannot understand ethical language. Without the experience of the Christian life, Christian theology cannot be made meaningful, because it is impossible to translate its terms into the terms of another game without distorting their meaning. Linguistic analysis made a useful contribution to the understanding of Christian communication when it pointed out that language gets its meaning from its use in life. As Wittgenstein points out, if we are in a strange country, with entirely strange traditions, we may master the language but still we do not *understand* the people. When language is uprooted from the life in which it grows, it withers and dies. There is no way to share Christian language without sharing the Christian life. There is no way to analyze the language game of Christian theology without analyzing the Christian way of life.

The traditional language of the church sounds strange today, and the apologist must translate that language. This is what Christian preaching and thinking has done in every age. Today the Christian apologist is tempted to try to translate Christian terms into terms of other language games, but when he does this he does not translate; he loses the Christian faith. The fact is that every attempt to translate the faith runs into the danger that it may end up substituting an alien system for the gospel.

NOTES

1. Willem F. Zuurdeeg, *An Analytical Philosophy of Religion.*
2. J. C. C. Smart, "The Existence of God," *New Essays in Philosophical Theology,* edited by Antony G. N. Flew and Alas-

dair C. MacIntyre (London: SCM Press, Ltd., 1955), p. 50.

3. William Blackstone, *The Problem of Religious Knowledge* (Prentice-Hall, Inc., 1963), esp. pp. 125–171.

4. *Ibid.*, p. 130.

II B

EXPERIENCE AND VERIFICATION

Frederick Ferré

I have noticed, in my reading of current theological literature, that the philosophically crucial notion of verification by experience tends to be employed by some theologians with a certain recklessness. Such recklessness (alas!) introduces needless confusions into the already immensely subtle and complex issues that theologians must wrestle with. Paul van Buren, for example, makes extensive reference to the notion of verification and to something that he calls "the Verification Principle" in his arguments. But his use of such terminology is almost unrecognizably different from the use made of it by the linguistic philosophers he purports to be following. This makes it difficult for philosophers to understand *The Secular Meaning of the Gospel,* and in consequence some philosophers may fail to take its theological content as seriously as perhaps we should. A similar problem—though differently manifested—seems to run through Professor Moreau's essay, "Theology and Language." My first aim, then, will simply be to attempt a clarification that will prevent his general cognitivist position (which, if I understand it, I consider constructive) from riding off to the battlefield with its armor needlessly askew.

I

One strong indication that something is askew is Professor Moreau's assertion that "all other statements [than analytic or synthetic ones], being exempt from the verification process, may be true or false, but there is no way of showing them to be either." This is, however, exactly what *cannot* be the case on the verification principle of meaning. Linguistic expressions that are logically exempt from the verification process are, by virtue of that very fact, held to be devoid of cognitive significance; they are not genuine "statements" at all. I believe that this verificationist position is wrongheaded, for a variety of reasons, but it is important not to blunt its impact by presenting it as less radical than in fact it is. Thus by treating the verification principle in such a strange fashion, Professor Moreau makes us wonder what, precisely, he means by "verification."

The wonder is intensified by other passages that are still more important in the formulation of Professor Moreau's own position. He tells us that: "the statements adopted by the Councils were meant to be *tests* of the language of systematic theology. These statements provided [*sic*] the verification of theological discourse, but instead of being [*sic*] a publicly available corpus [*sic*] of experience, they pointed to the religious experience of a definable community."

There is room for considerable puzzlement here.

a. In what way can a Council's statements, which are themselves theological discourse, function as the *tests* (in any philosophically interesting sense) of theological discourse? I can understand how official ecclesiastical formularies could be stipulated as *norms of linguistic correctness;* and in this sense Council statements can be said to be syntactical tests. But of course this is quite a different sense of "test" from the sense relevant to the experiential "testing procedures" of the verifying process. This latter sense, however, does seem to be what Professor Moreau has in mind when he introduces in this passage the question of experience. Thus I propose an amendment. "These statements," he tells us, "provided the verification of theological discourse." I assume that we should now read this as "made *possible* the verification, etc.," rather than "provided," since we have already seen that language can *provide* sufficient verification

for other language only if we transpose the meaning of "verification" into a purely syntactical key.

b. Very well, how do the statements of the Council "make
possible" the experiential verification of theological discourse?
(1) We are told that this is not by "being a publicly available
corpus of experience"—which surely goes without saying, since
experiential statements do not function, as statements, by *being*
experience but by *referring* to experience. And in any event it
is not clear to me what a "corpus" of experience would be. Thus
I propose a paraphrase; Professor Moreau is interested in denying
that conciliar statements make possible the verification of theological discourse by referring to publicly available kinds of
experience. (2) How then? They function by pointing "to the
religious experience of a definable community," we are told.
But this, too, raises problems if we have already ruled out "publicly available" experience. How "public" is "public"? If a
definable *community* can be said to share some kind of experience, must we not grant that such experience is rather public?
What, in any event, *is* "public experience," and how important
is the publicity of experience, in any case, to the verification
of assertions?

Other passages in Professor Moreau's paper indicate that the
distinctions between experiences and assertions that we need
even to ask this basic question are blurred in his treatment of
the subject. He says: "We must develop some criteria for determining the validity of one construct of theological assertions
over another, or a method of distinguishing between real or
claimed perception and mere hallucination." Does Professor
Moreau, then, assume that these two tasks are roughly synonymous? So it appears, since the great differences between setting
up standards for *determining the evidential power of experience,* on the one hand, and developing criteria for *testing assertions,* on the other hand, are never explicitly noted. Again, Professor Moreau declares, a little later, that what is required
is "the development of canons of verification to determine the
validity or invalidity of key religious experiences, expressed

symbolically, around which an understanding of all experience is organized." This proposal, however, muddles together the symbolization of experience with the experience symbolized, thus unfortunately confusing that which *is verified* with that which *does the verifying.* Little wonder, then, that some profess to find not much of constructive value in theological attempts to utilize techniques of analytical philosophy; unless treated with great care, the light that shineth in the darkness may make the flickering shadows even deeper black.

II

To this point I have been attempting to lay bare a difficulty that I believe threatens the usefulness of Professor Moreau's essay. I have endeavored to clarify the difference between (*a*) the problem of distinguishing hallucinations from trustworthy experiences and (*b*) the problem of marshaling support, by means of such criteria as adequacy and coherence, for what Professor Moreau calls "a religious affirmation, as a construct of related assertions." Now, I should like to touch briefly on both these topics separately. First, I shall venture an opinion on what must characterize any experience that can be important in the verifying process; and, secondly, I shall acknowledge a serious dilemma that confronts anyone like Professor Moreau—or myself —who may wish to test religious assertions by the criteria he suggests.

a. *Experience as evidence.* First, how would one go about determining the "validity or invalidity" of religious—or any—experiences? We may as well defuse complaints over Professor Moreau's use of the term "validity" in this context, if it bothers the purist who points out that this term is properly applied to arguments rather than to experiences, by substituting some other expression. "Veridicality," is the dreadful term blessed by psychological usage. How do veridical perceptions, then, differ from hallucinations?

One simple answer is that veridical perceptions are good evidence for assertions about what is so; hallucinations are not. This is not to say that hallucinations are "not so." Of course they *occur,* but they lack evidential power.

But this was not all we were asking for: granting that hallucinations, once they have been identified as such, cannot be used to verify anything beyond themselves, how can we tell the difference between hallucinations and veridical perceptions?

There are a number of tests. One is to check for regularity of sequence within our experience (Were my senses deceiving me?—I must look again under similar circumstances); another is to check for regularity of interconnection between various types of experience (You think you are seeing snakes?—can you hear hissing or touch scaly bodies?); but the crucial test for the evidential power of an experience remains the possibility of communicability (Am I going crazy?—or do *you* see what *I* see?). The crucial test of veridicality in experience, that is, is its *publicity.* Without publicity, indeed, an experience should not be considered to have evidential power even to the private individual having that experience.

This is a hard saying, and frequently misunderstood. I am *not* arguing that only sense experience makes good evidence, though the regularities of sequence, interconnection, and communicable structure that typify sense experience usually make it excellent evidence. Nor am I forgetting that everyone's experience is *his* experience and so, in a trivial sense, all experience is "private." It is the presence in some types of experience of communicable structure that counts for its publicity. Sheerly "private" experience, in this sense, would merely be idiosyncratic.

The fact that I used the expression *"sheerly* private" in my last sentence suggests that I believe that there may be degrees of publicity and privacy. This is indeed my conviction. Even with respect to sense experience there are notorious degrees of communicability. Vision probably allows for more qualitative discriminations than any other sense; smell, in human beings, even in professional perfume testers, is comparatively devoid of communicable structures. Nonsensory responses to music or painting are even more so. But this is precisely to underline a point that I consider most important: It is impossible to rule a priori on what the content of evidentially powerful experience may be like. If sensory experience lacks the marks of good evidence, it must be set aside. If extrasensory experience manifests the marks of good evidence, then it must be counted just as "public," just as useful in the business of verifying assertions, as similarly warranted experience from other sources. It may turn out to be the case, for example, that certain very unusual experiences regularly associated with the ingestion of L.S.D. or other psychedelic materials may become "publicly available" to the community of those who have taken the drug. I have had a fascinating session with this drug, and now find that I can communicate fairly well with others who have had L.S.D., at least about certain significant structural aspects of the experience. And this will increase if a psychedelic vocabulary can gradually be forged.

This is, of course, only an example; I would hate to introduce any red herrings into the discussion. But it is an apt example, I think, because the drug experience is often compared with religious experiences. Careful empirical work has shown that its soul-shaking effects may with literal justice be termed "mystical." We find also a community of experiences, in both cases, among those who struggle to speak of what our ordinary vocabularies do not permit. This might, indeed, be one of the most important applications of psychedelic drugs: they allow people to have for themselves kinds of experience that they never dreamed possible for themselves or others—and to help people, in consequence, rid themselves of some of their smug prejudices.

b. *Theories and evidence.* If experience—even odd kinds of experience—may count as evidence only when it manifests certain intersubjective regularities, the need for evidence itself is always relative to assertions, theories, or claims. And here, as I promised earlier, I must confess a final problem. I am not going to try to deal here with the complex and much controverted issues that set my problem. I shall simply assume, with Professor Moreau, that at least one of the functions of theological discourse is to make assertions about what is the case; and I shall further assume, also with Professor Moreau, that there are criteria appropriate to the appraisal of the success attained in this function, of which I believe two very important ones are (1) the Whiteheadian understanding of the *coherence* of the propositions within a theoretical theological structure, of which Professor Moreau makes little explicit use (but which he clearly accepts, e.g., p. 70), and (2) the *adequacy* of the theoretical theological structure as a whole to the job of interpreting and ordering the whole range of human experience. That is a lot to assume in one great gulp, but I must beg your indulgence; I have attempted to work out the justification of such assumptions in some detail elsewhere.

Having taken this rather basic stance, however, I find myself in a genuine dilemma. I have here been urging a more tolerant and inclusive view on what might count as evidentially powerful experience; and I have accepted the criterion of adequacy to all such evidentially powerful experience as constituting one of the most important measures of the cognitive success of a theological theory. But at the very same time I have agreed that another supremely important job of a theological theory is to make coherent sense out of life and life's experiences. And here is my dilemma: The criterion of coherence among assertions tends toward neatness; the criterion of adequacy to experience tends toward messiness. I say that I want both. What shall I do?

There are several possible responses to this question. The first would be to deny that experience—at least evidentially powerful experience—is in fact mixed up in messiness. But this Apollonian highroad is not an escape open to me. I cannot bring myself to explain away the murky depths of things that mystics grope for; I cannot dismiss as insignificant the wild, the mad, the creative (or the demonic) heights and depths that break neat patterns and shatter familiar coherences. There are too many others, in too many times and places, who have found such experience evidentially powerful. I cannot in honesty afford to purchase coherence at the price of adequacy to these experiential facts.

A second response to my dilemma would be to deny that coherence is particularly desirable. But this unkempt Dionysian way is barred for me too. Pattern, order, neatness, are not everything; but sheer anarchy destroys the value even of spontaneity. Life demands some measure of integration or it destroys itself. A life divided against itself is doomed. Health and wholeness are essentially, not accidentally, related. And therefore there must be no abandonment of the integrative and unifying role of coherence in the theological theory if the faith it structures is to give us life and give it more abundantly.

Where are we then? If adequacy to sorts of experience (which we must not dismiss) destroys coherence among our formulations (which we may not despise), how can we find comfort for our metaphysical yearning? Perhaps there will be no immediate comfort. *I ask that this possibility be carefully considered,* since in this moment in history, at least, we seem required to live uncomfortably in the tension of this situation. None of our standard cosmic coherences, our traditional metaphysical schemes, our theological orthodoxies, are rich enough. None of our familiar attempts to be adequate are yet sufficiently integral. The demands are felt; and these felt demands are justified. But we have no obvious answer, no "consensus" solution to assuage the demand. The "standard brand" solutions have lost their former "aptness."

Perhaps this is the most characteristic trait of modern men: We are disaffected with our traditional cosmic answers but we are also unpersuaded by the scoffers—be they positivist or obscurantist —who urge that the desire for such answers is misguided or inauthentic. We stand, therefore, and wait. But while we wait we need also to work at sharpening the tools that will help us measure the aptness of new or reformed answers when they come—since candidates for our commitments will come, are coming, have been coming, as surely as nature abhors a vacuum. Who knows? The winning candidate may already be among us, incognito. This is finally why it is so important to do what Professor Moreau urges, and to do it clearly. Here is one useful way, at any rate, to make the best of the present moment of uncertainty and confusion: by pushing back, if possible, the boundaries of significant human experience, and by preparing to recognize theoretical adequacy and coherence in any future theology that may succeed in combining them more fully than in the past. May it come soon! And may we be ready!

III

THE NEW METAPHYSICS
AND THEOLOGY

William A. Christian

I

The process of living as human beings is complex, like the weaving of a web from many strands, not only because the world is full of many things—more, indeed, than are dreamed of in our philosophies—but also, and mainly, because we ourselves are moved to think and act in different ways.

We think about our moral obligations and ideals and responsibilities in a way somewhat different from the way we think about electrons and genes and reflexes. We think about sets, and prime numbers, and curves in a way somewhat different from that in which we think about intimations of the holy, or the chief end of man, or a way of salvation. We think about bridge-building and computer-designing in a way different from the way we think about poems and paintings and musical compositions. Our processes of thinking and acting in these different kinds of cases have different roots.

Yet it is one and the same man who thinks and acts in these different ways, from these different roots. So it is not strange that connections and interactions occur. An interest in music leads to an interest in mathematics. In the course of discovering what happened in history, we discover also something about ourselves. What we learn about the causes of poverty teaches us something about our responsibilities.

We neglect such connections and interactions at our peril, the peril of impoverishing our existence. And when we not only neglect them but guard against them, as we are sometimes tempted to do in order to simplify our lives, we do so at an even greater peril, namely, of becoming not one person but two or many.

Now such contrasts and connections and interactions may themselves become objects of reflection. Then we are engaging in a certain kind of philosophical activity, namely, critical philosophy, which may be specialized as the philosophy of science, the philosophy of morals, or of art or of religion. It is in this vein that we ask how interaction is possible between metaphysical thinking and theological thinking, with a view, later on, to the new metaphysics. This is one way to try to understand the unity as well as the multiplicity of our thinking and being.

In asking how interaction between metaphysics and theology is possible, I am assuming that each stands on its own feet, that each has some logical basis which is relatively independent of the basis of the other. If this were not the case, then at least one of the following propositions would be true:

a. Metaphysics has no logical basis at all. In the past fifty years there has been a great deal of argument for this view.

b. Theology has no logical basis at all. It is perhaps a productive art, like poetry.

c. Metaphysics is a branch of theology.

d. Theology is a branch of metaphysics. It has no principles of judgment to appeal to except metaphysical principles of judgment.

So I am assuming that none of these propositions is true. I do not plan to offer explicit arguments against any of them, though my discussion may indirectly furnish some such reasons.[1] I shall assume that metaphysics has a logical basis, that theology has a logical basis, that metaphysics is not a branch of theology, and that theology is not a branch of metaphysics. Assuming all this, how is interaction between theology and metaphysics possible?

II

Consider the question: What sorts of things are there? For this question comes close to the root of metaphysical thinking. I do not say this is the only metaphysical question. But it is certainly one of the oldest questions in our own philosophical tradition, and it recurs with impressive regularity throughout the history of that tradition. To see the point of this question, consider first some remarks which would not be responsive to it. These remarks I shall mention would not be wrong answers; they would not be answers at all. They would miss the point of the question.

Someone might say: "Well, there is you, and there is me, and the desk, and the Archangel Michael, and Emory University," and so on. The world is full of a number of things. But the question asks not what things there are, but what sorts of things there are. A list of things would not do; it would not meet the point of the question.

Or someone might say: "Well, there are chairs and tables and people and books and mountains," and so on. Now this certainly tells us about sorts of things, not just about things one by one. But common sense, though we cannot do without it—and metaphysicians especially cannot do well without it—is not metaphysics. So if we can see why our question asks for something more than commonsense answers, we can see farther into the nature and roots of metaphysical thinking.

Put bluntly, the reason why we are not satisfied with commonsense answers is that this is something we already know. What we want is more light on what we know. This is the motive for speculative ontology. This is the reason why Aristotle says, in his *Metaphysics*, that the great question we ask when we seek wisdom is, What is being? and then, wrestling with this question, produce various lists of categories: substances, qualities, relations, etc. This is why Descartes introduces his distinction between thinking things and extended things—which, as he develops it, is by no means a commonsense distinction. This is why Leibniz introduces the concept of monads, which is far from being commonsensical. And this is why Whitehead begins his systematic construction with a list of categories of existence (actual entities, eternal objects, prehensions, nexus, etc.).

All these are various answers to the speculative question: What sorts of things are there? And in all these cases the invention (or discovery) of categories is for the sake of illuminating our prespeculative experience. They are not intended to supplant commonsense categories. Thus speculative discourse is not a substitute for ordinary discourse, for the way we speak in the practical affairs of life, though in the course of time it may modify ordinary discourse. Instead, it gives interpretations of the experiences we express in ordinary discourse and in scientific discourse and in other ways, with a view to understanding them better.

Out of this basic question of speculative philosophy other questions arise, such as: What are the structural relations between things of these sorts? Thus, in addition to categories of existence, speculative philosophy develops categories of explanation, in the form of rules for the systematic use of the categories of existence.

Now, let us turn from metaphysics, or, as I have been calling it, speculative philosophy, to theology.

III

It is possible to take the term "theology" as a name for a branch of metaphysics. It used to be said that just as rational anthropology is the study of the nature of man, and cosmology is the study of the structure of the world, so rational (or natural) theology is the study of the nature and attributes of God. But from my opening remarks you will have gathered that I mean to construe theology in a different way. I shall construe theology as a certain enterprise within religious thought.

Within any religious community that becomes reflective about its beliefs, there develops an attempt to explicate these beliefs and to relate them to one another. Furthermore, for any religious community there is some starting point for thought. There is some particular sort of experience or some particular historical event (for example, the enlightenment of Gotama or the life and death and resurrection of Christ) to which the thought and activity of the community is a response. The systematic explication of the doctrines of the community will proceed from this starting point. This gives the enterprise its unity and continuity.

Now, while we can say that in any reflective religious community there is a systematic explication of doctrines, we might not want to call this "theology" in every case, because some religious communities—for example, Buddhism—are not theistic in any clear sense. So we might want to restrict the term "theology" to mean the systematic explication of doctrines in theistic religious communities.

Theology in this sense has its roots in religion, and a particular theology has its roots in a particular religion. So we should ask ourselves whether there is some question or family of questions to which various systems of religious doctrine are addressed. If so, this would enable us to arrive at some analogies and contrasts with speculative ontology.

As we study various religious systems in their theory and practice, it seems that they all involve pointing to something which has supreme significance for human life. They point to something which is holy, or to some supreme goal of life, or to some chief end of man, or to the source of being and nonbeing, or to a way of freedom from inner bondage. So they can be construed as answers, not perhaps to some one question, but to some one of a family of questions. And we can express the common intent of these questions in the following way: What is it that is of central and ultimate significance for human life? Let us use the letter P as a variable, and take "What is it that is P?" as the form of a basic religious question, allowing as values of this variable various religious predicates, examples of which I have mentioned, such as "holy," "the supreme goal of life," "the source of being and nonbeing," and others.

IV

If this is so, then we can reframe our initial question in the
following way. We asked how interaction between metaphysics
and theology was possible. Now, if we take speculative ontology
as basic to metaphysics, and if we construe theology as I have
done, then we can ask: How is interaction possible between,
on the one hand, an enterprise that answers the question, What
sorts of things are there? and, on the other hand, an enterprise
that answers the question, What is it that is of central and ultimate significance for human life? or better, using our variable,
a question of the form, What is it that is P?

At this point someone might say that the basic religious
question involved in some theology presupposes some ontology,
and that in this way theology presupposes metaphysics. For it
seems that in order to decide what P is true of, we must first
have some idea of what there is. Before we can point to something as having central or ultimate significance for human life,
it seems we must already have some range of entities from which
we select.

But caution is needed here. The basic question of speculative
ontology, we said, is, What sorts of things are there? And we
can have a range of individuals without having a range of sorts
of individuals. We can think of this, that, and that, and the other
thing without thinking of sorts of things in a speculative way.

Certainly, a great deal of theology reflects a relatively un-
speculative way of thinking, in our sense of "speculative." And
some theologians have said that this is a good thing. They have
argued that their enterprise does not depend on speculative
ontology. And, as I have said, on this point I think they are right.

But we could say that theology does not depend on speculative
ontology for its being without denying that speculative ontology
can contribute to the well-being of theology. We could say that
the basis of each of these enterprises is different. The question
at the basis of each can be intelligibly asked independently of
the question at the basis of the other. There could be speculative

philosophers who do not ask a question of the form, What is it that is P? And there could be theologians who do not ask, What sorts of things are there? in a speculative way. But still a theologian might explicate the doctrines of his faith in relation to some speculative ontology that seemed to him to be true, as indeed many theologians have done.

Now, let us consider a problem in speculative ontology. Suppose we have constructed (or discovered) a set of categories to denote the sorts of things there are. Then how do we know we have not left out something, something that does not fit into any of these categories? For example, the perennial question about Descartes's ontology is this: There are material things, and there are minds. If this is an adequate set of ontological categories, then we would not find anything that is neither a body nor a mind, nor a proper combination (according to his categories of explanation) of things of these sorts. But are the things we call persons interpretable in this way? Or has Descartes left out, not in intention but in effect, something that does not fit into his categoreal scheme?

I do not want to argue this particular question. I only want to point out a consequence if the second answer is correct. If there are things that do not fit into Descartes's scheme, then his ontology is inadequate and hence untrue. If we still ask the speculative question, some other answer would have to be found.

Now, some theologians have claimed, with respect to this or that ontology, that a similar situation obtains. They say that something has been left out; there is something which does not fit into the categories of these ontologies. Further, they have claimed that this is something of very great importance, indeed of supreme importance.

Of course, these claims would have to be made good. They would have to be supported in appropriate ways. It would have to be argued, first, that such an entity does in fact exist, and, secondly, that the categories of the scheme in question (that of Aristotle, or of Descartes, or of Whitehead, for example) do not yield an adequate interpretation of it. Here some nice questions arise that I shall not even try to untangle. What sort of interpretation is adequate? What sort of interpretation does speculative ontology claim to be able to give? What sort of interpretation is appropriate to speculative ontology? It would be wrong to expect too much.

So far, there is nothing antiphilosophical or even unphilosophical about theological objections to particular ontologies. Indeed, the possibility that something has been left out has to be allowed, and risked, by any speculative philosopher. Otherwise, there seems no way of testing the adequacy of his ontology. By these objections, therefore, a theologian will contribute indirectly to the progress of speculative philosophy if he can argue his case.

Now, a theologian might claim not only that a particular ontology is thus untrue but also that a large number of ontologies, indeed all those with which he is at present acquainted, are thus untrue, since none of them yields an interpretation of the entity in question. Even so, this would not yet be a claim that all possible ontologies are untrue. The moral would be only that a better ontology needs to be constructed. In other words, the kind of objection I have been considering so far is not at all inimical to speculative philosophy. If this sort of objection is not possible, in principle, then progress in speculative philosophy is not possible. So this sort of objection should count as a constructive interaction between theology and speculative philosophy.

But theologians have sometimes made another kind of objection to speculative philosophy. Sometimes they have gone farther and claimed that no possible ontology could yield an interpretation of the entity to which they refer. This unrestricted objection would indeed be inimical to speculative philosophy, and would be disastrous to that enterprise if, but only if, it could be made good—if, that is to say, it could be shown that such an entity exists, and that no possible ontology could yield an interpretation of it. I have one comment on this sort of objection.

Saying that the concept of God falls under some category of

being might seem offensive to religious sensibility for the following reason. Often, to classify something is to downgrade it.
For example:

John is not particularly fond of Jane; she's just another girl.
He's a politician, after all, like the rest of them.
The earth is only one of a number of planets in the universe.

So, saying that God is a being or a substance or an actual entity
might be taken, by association, as a way of diminishing the
importance of God or of denying his uniqueness, though this
may be neither the intent nor the logical effect of such speculative propositions themselves.

For when we speak of God in a religious way, the point of
speaking about him is not to classify him but to call attention
to the difference between him and all else. But this need not
imply that God is utterly unlike all other beings. And if not,
then those respects (if any) in which he is like other things
would be defining properties of classes of which God and other
things are members. Though we may in this way class God
with other entities in certain respects (for example, as active),
we may also deny that he is only a member of the class of active
beings, and likewise, for any other class one might choose. We
mark him off from all else. The use of speculative categories
in speaking of God is compatible with acknowledging his
transcendence.

So far I have been arguing that it is possible for speculative
philosophy and theology to interact in a fruitful way. Theological propositions may take on speculative import, and speculative propositions may take on theological import, as I have
tried to show. Still, speculative propositions must be judged by
speculative principles of judgment and theological propositions
must be judged by theological principles of judgment, even
though the two sets of principles may overlap.

Sometimes I wonder at the assurance with which philosophers,
speculative or analytical, tell us what the concept of God (or
the Christian concept of God, or the Judeo-Christian concept

of God) must include and exclude. As I think of the history of theology in our civilization, it does not seem a simple matter to delimit that concept. Further, sometimes I wonder whether philosophers know when they cross the boundary between speculative philosophy and theology. For the Jewish doctrine of God is surely a doctrine of Jewish theology, and the Christian doctrine of God is surely a doctrine of Christian theology. What these doctrines say, or ought to say, is certainly a matter for theological argument according to theological principles of judgment.

I am not suggesting that the boundary should not be crossed. On the contrary, boundary-crossing may be a very good thing. None of us is just a philosopher, or just a theologian, or just a scientist, or just a moralist. We are men. For example, if some moral suggestion should occur to a scientist while he is engaged with a problem of physics, let him develop the suggestion in relation to moral problems. But let him realize that he is crossing a boundary, and let him submit the theory he develops to appropriate principles of moral judgment. Let him not confuse it with the theories of physics with which he had been engaged. In a similar way, if a speculative philosopher comes to be interested in the Christian concept of God, let him understand that theological questions have to be settled in accord with theological principles of judgment, principles derived from the starting point of Christian theology.

V

Now, let us turn to one of the most important speculative philosophers of this century, Alfred North Whitehead. How and why is the concept of God in Whitehead's speculative philosophy important? First, I shall mention some wrong reasons for thinking that it is important:

a. Sometimes it is supposed that since Whitehead's philosophy has been influenced by modern science, we have here a concept of God to which modern science gives direct support. This is a mistake. Between a system of speculative philosophy and the concepts and conclusions of modern science there is, at best, only an indirect relation.

b. Again, sometimes it is supposed that we ought to take Whitehead's concept of God as a direct contribution to Christian theology. I think this is also a mistake, for I would argue that the relation between any speculative system and Christian theology is, again, only an indirect relation.[2] I shall return to this point at the end.

The real reasons why the concept of God in Whitehead's philosophy is important are as follows:

a. This concept is an integral part of a system of speculative philosophy. In this way it is unlike certain concepts of God which have only an accidental or tenuous relation to the philosophical systems in which they appear. It seems clear that the concept of God in Whitehead's philosophy is required by his cosmology. It is firmly embedded in his conceptual scheme.

b. This system is itself philosophically important for three reasons taken in conjunction. It is remarkably original; it is very rich in its applications—it is relevant for example to mathematics, to natural science, to epistemology, to the history of philosophy, to practical experience, to aesthetic judgment, to the history of civilization, to education, and to religion; and finally, it is highly articulate in its logical structure, as we might expect from a mind long disciplined by rigorous thought.

c. This concept of God bears a strong family resemblance to those conceptions of God which have dominated philosophical theology in the history of Western civilization, for example, those of Aristotle, Plotinus, Augustine, Aquinas, Spinoza, and Leibniz. It is sometimes said that Whitehead ought not to have used the term "God" for the primordial and everlasting actual entity. I believe that this judgment is based either on a superficial understanding of Whitehead's concept or on an indefensible view of the use of terms in language.

I have said in passing that Whitehead's concept of God is required by his concept of the actual world. Without developing that point further, let me call attention to three other features of Whitehead's concept of God: how this concept requires the concept of an actual world; how the world makes a difference in God; and how God is unchangeable.[3]

a. *How the concept of God in Whitehead's philosophy requires the concept of an actual world.* Whitehead says: "The purpose of God is the attainment of value in the temporal world."[4] And since the purpose of God is intrinsic to his nature, not extrinsic to it, the unity of the divine experience requires the existence of an actual world. The actuality of God does not require *this* actual world, or any other particular actual world as such. The point is only that some state of temporal things or other is required by Whitehead's concept of God.

The issue could be posed in this way: Let us suppose—though we cannot imagine it—that nothing finite exists. We would not just be supposing that *we* do not exist, or that the world as we know it does not exist, but that nothing finite whatever exists. Then, with this supposition, Whitehead's concept of God would not make sense.

b. *How, in Whitehead's concept of God, the world makes a difference in God.* God prehends the world as it is and for what it is. Now, the world as it exists today is very different from the world as it existed a million years ago. Many events, some of them of crucial importance, have occurred since then.

Now, if real changes occur in the world, and if God prehends the world as it is and for what it is, then events in space and time must make a difference in what God prehends. And since his prehensions of the world are not merely external relations but intrinsic to his being, changes in the world must make some difference in God. With changes in the states of things, the possibilities God envisages are ordered in new and different ways. Thus his action is relevant to each new situation. One application of this concept would be as follows. What God could do for people who had read Hegel and Nietzsche, *or* people who had learned from experience in a certain way, would be different from what God could do for people who had not learned from experience in that way. Such a fact would pose new problems, and also open new opportunities.

c. *How God is unchangeable, according to Whitehead's concept of God.* There are two respects in which, according to Whitehead's theory, nothing could make a difference in God. First, nothing that occurs can diminish God's actuality. Suppose, for example, that human life should cease to exist on this planet. Still, on Whitehead's conception of God and the world, this would not diminish the actuality of God. Suppose further that the value of entropy should increase, so that instead of the complex structures of organic and inorganic material objects as we know them, the universe would be reduced to wisps of undifferentiated matter drifting about in empty space. Even so, on Whitehead's conception of God and the world, the actuality of God would be undiminished. The pattern of the divine experience would be affected, since God prehends the world for what it happens to be, but his actuality would be undiminished.

Second, nothing could weaken or deflect God's aim at maximum realization of possibilities. His purpose as well as his actuality would remain unshaken. He is the ground of creativity for any situation whatever. Something can always be achieved. But what, and how much, can be achieved depends, in part, on what the environment of a given event permits.

VI

Many theologians, both in the history of Judaism and in the history of Christianity, have explicated their religious doctrines in the framework of Platonic speculative philosophy, because they thought that Platonism, as a speculative philosophy, was true. So it will advance our understanding of how interaction between theology and metaphysics is possible, and also put the outcome of Whitehead's philosophy in a clearer light, if we contrast some of Whitehead's doctrines with some Platonic doctrines.

When I speak of Platonic doctrines, I am not referring to

what Plato said but to certain historical developments from what he said. As you know, Platonism entered the main streams of Western religious thought by way of Philo, Plotinus, the pseudo-Dionysius and other Neoplatonists. The history of some of these doctrines has been traced and examined in Arthur O. Lovejoy's fine book, *The Great Chain of Being.*[5]

a. One of these doctrines is that all things have their unity in God. That is to say, each thing has its proper unity only in God. This doctrine gets expressed in many ways and undergoes various transformations in the history of Western thought. Sometimes it exists alongside other views with which it is not altogether in harmony. Since the reality of a thing, in this tradition, is closely linked to its unity, one implication of this doctrine is that finite things are not really real. Some alternative ways in which it is expressed in various systems are as follows:

All things other than God are emanations from God.

Finite things have their being only by participation in God.

All things other than God are modes of the divine substance.

Whitehead's doctrine, which stands in contrast with this Platonic doctrine, may be put in the following way: God is necessary to the existence of temporal actual entities. But each temporal actual entity has its own subjective unity as an experiencing subject, and this unity is fully realized in its own "satisfaction." In this sense every finite actual entity is complete. It is as actual as anything can be. Further, each actual occasion contributes its finite achievement to the unity of God's experience. So Whitehead views existence not as a great chain of being but as a rhythmical process in which both God and finite actual entities are real and effective.

b. A second Platonic doctrine, with which the outcome of Whitehead's theory may be compared, is as follows: All possibilities for the world are actualized. All the possible modes of being are exhausted in actuality. Hence, when we look to Platonism for an interpretation of history, we find, at best, a cyclical view of history. Nothing really new can happen because all the possibilities are eternally realized in God.

The Whiteheadian contrast to this doctrine is as follows: There is an inexhaustible multiplicity of pure possibilities ("eternal objects"). God envisages all these possibilities and aims at maximal realization of them in the temporal world. But no state of affairs can ever fully actualize all possibilities. For in relation to any given state of affairs some possibilities will be incompatible with others. Hence, genuine novelty in the temporal world is always possible, and God is the lure toward novel forms of being.

    c. Consider a third Platonic doctrine: Ecstatic union with God is the supreme goal of life. This follows both from the first Platonic doctrine and from the second Platonic doctrine. It follows from the first doctrine because one must be united with God to be oneself. One must go "up," so to speak, to find one's own unity of being. It follows also from the second doctrine because, since there are no unrealized possibilities for the future, there is nowhere else to go.

    In contrast, it follows from Whitehead's theory of God and the world that the aim of life is the achievement of novel temporal satisfactions. These satisfactions are made possible by God, and awareness of God may enter into these satisfactions, so that life includes "a mode of satisfaction deeper than joy or sorrow."[6]

VII

Whitehead made his own sense of indebtedness to Plato, and his objections to Platonism, clear and explicit. But his thought has roots in the Christian tradition as well, and it is important to consider the outcome of his theory in relation to Christian theology. Instead of comparing the outcome of Whitehead's theory with some Christian doctrines, I shall approach this topic in a different way.

    The Christian tradition is a different sort of thing from the Platonic tradition. It is a "tradition" in a somewhat different sense. The concepts of the Christian tradition are concepts that arise and have their primary use within a particular community, in a sense of "community" in which it would not be quite proper to speak of a Platonic community. Further, the members of this community live by and proclaim the universal significance of a particular historical event, and its theologians explicate and develop this significance.

Now, in a given historical situation, such as our own, this development of Christian doctrines will occur in a particular intellectual context, of which the theologian may be more or less aware. It is significant that some of the great theologians of the past were not only aware of the movements of thought in their times but were, further, men whose experience had been illuminated by non-Christian concepts, as for example, Augustine's experience had been illuminated by Neoplatonism before he became a Christian, and as Aquinas' experience was illuminated by Aristotle's philosophy of nature. The problem for these theologians is, then, as follows: How does the Christian gospel transform these non-Christian concepts? How does it illuminate these other illuminations of experience?

Now it seems to me that the outcome of Whitehead's theory of God and the world is somewhat nearer to the Christian outlook on the world than to the Platonic tradition, though this is debatable. But the main point I wish to make is that the kind of problem posed for Christian theology by Whitehead's philosophy is similar to the problems posed by Neoplatonism in the fifth century and Aristotelianism in the thirteenth century. Christian theology must develop from its own roots, but its life may be fertilized and invigorated by influences that penetrate the soil in which it grows. It may be that in our time Whitehead's philosophy will be such an influence.

No doubt some theologians will go on adapting Whitehead to their purposes without understanding his problems and his solutions. This way of despoiling the philosophers, as the ancient Hebrews despoiled the Egyptians, taking jewels of silver and gold, and raiment, is an old theological habit. But often the jewels are displayed in bad taste and the raiment does not fit. When theologians appropriate and make use of speculative theories, they do less than justice both to speculative philosophy and to their own discipline. Augustine did not make use of Neoplatonism. He was a Neoplatonic philosopher who had become a Christian theologian. "I had sought strenuously after that gold which thou didst allow thy people to take from Egypt, since wherever it was it was thine." *(Conf.* VII. ix. 15). Aquinas did not make use of Aristotle. He was a Christian theologian who was also an Aristotelian philosopher.

Some theologians, including some very able ones, are not, in their own experience as men, moved to ask speculative questions. Some find such questions trivial and uninteresting; some find them unintelligible or confusing. For such theologians speculative questions are not real questions.

Other theologians, in their own experience as men, are moved to ask speculative questions, with a view to better understanding of themselves and their world. To them, qua speculative philosophers, Whitehead[7] has something important to say. And as they go on being both theologians and philosophers, vital and productive interactions between these different enterprises of the human spirit may occur. But such interactions cannot be altogether contrived, and they cannot be entirely predicted.

NOTES

1. See William A. Christian, "Some Uses of Reason" in Ivor Leclerc, ed., *The Relevance of Whitehead* (The Macmillan Company, 1961); and William A. Christian, *Meaning and Truth in Religion* (Princeton University Press, 1964).

2. Here I am in agreement with John B. Cobb, Jr., in *A Christian Natural Theology* (The Westminster Press, 1965), in respect of what he says about "Christian theology proper" on p. 277.

3. See William A. Christian, *An Interpretation of Whitehead's Metaphysics* (Yale University Press, 1959), Part III; and "The

Concept of God as a Derivative Notion," in William L. Reese and Eugene Freeman, eds., *Process and Divinity* (The Open Court Publishing Company, 1964).

4. Alfred North Whitehead, *Religion in the Making* (The Macmillan Company, 1926), p. 100.

5. Arthur O. Lovejoy, *The Great Chain of Being* (Harvard University Press, 1936).

6. Alfred North Whitehead, *Adventures of Ideas* (The Macmillan Company, 1933), p. 221.

7. And other philosophers, Paul Weiss and Charles Hartshorne, for example, who have approached speculative philosophy in somewhat similar ways.

III A

WHITEHEAD: *REDEVIVUS?*

OR *ABSCONDITUS?*

Stanley R. Hopper

I should feel easier about Professor Christian's advocacy of Whitehead's "New Metaphysics" for theology today had he begun with Whitehead's own dictum that "philosophy never reverts to its old position after the shock of a great philosopher."[1] He might then have come forward with Whitehead as just such a philosopher, together with some sketch of that which is novel and radical in this new metaphysic and with a suggestion or two as to why it should commend itself especially for the "doing" of theology in these times. For Whitehead's point is that "a new idea introduces a new alternative."[2] As theologians, this is what we are interested in. What is the new idea to be found in Whitehead? What is the new alternative it makes possible for theology?

I am not at all sure that Professor Christian's paper makes either of these propositions clear. I do not wish to seem unappreciative, for what he has accomplished is considerable, and hedged in by almost insuperable problems of compression and definition. But it is possible that in failing to make the new idea and the new alternative clear, he has thrust Whitehead one step farther away from availability by inserting one more analytical interpretive screen between us and the distinguished philosopher he would commend.

Professor Christian's claims are modest, if not cautious. In the first half of his paper (secs. I–IV) he argues that there may be interaction between speculative philosophy and theology, and that speculative philosophy (Whitehead) may contribute fruitfully to such an enterprise. In the second half (secs. V, VI, VII) he brings Whitehead forward specifically as the speculative philosopher who can make such a contribution today because of (1) his concept of God, and (2) the grand scope of his philosophy, which commends comparison with those great systems of Western thinking which have been so useful in the past—Aristotle, Plotinus, Augustine, Aquinas, Spinoza, Leibniz. He is careful to observe that Christian theology must develop "from its own roots," but it may be "fertilized and invigorated by influences that penetrate the soil in which it grows." All of which seems to be formally correct, and so circumspectly qualified as to make discussion either arbitrary or simply gratuitous. Nevertheless, while there is not much to object to in the paper's formal proposals, there is perhaps much to differ with in terms of its mode of seeing these relationships, including its way of seeing Whitehead and his "speculative ontology."

To put the point directly, Whitehead's philosophy is *a philosophy of organism*, and this, with its corollaries and implications, is what is new about it. That Whitehead himself was fully aware of these implications seems plain. The development of Western thought in terms of "a static Absolute" has meant that "philosophy and theology have been saddled with the problem of deriving the historic world of change from a changeless world of ultimate reality. Our whole conception of knowledge has been vitiated."[3] Logic and mathematics conspired with "the science of a static universe": today it is necessary to translate the entire metaphysical tradition of Western philosophy from static to dynamic forms. This means historically that Whitehead dispenses with the methodological primacy of Aristotelian "substance" and "logic" in order to resume philosophic vision where Plato placed it—in the problem of becoming, being, and perishing. His entire philosophy might be said to be an amplification of the problem of the *Timaeus* as qualified by the new worldpicture derived from modern science.[4]

Process is thus characteristic, and becoming and perishing are its mysteries: what it takes from modern science is primarily the emergence of *novelty* in the world of actual entities. There is no other reality of a Platonic sort behind these entities to which their status must be referred. On the contrary, the forms of things must be detected from within the process, and our transcension of the process is always in the direction of creative advance, of a fresh concretion, which, while individual in itself, is nonetheless related to the whole. "God" is the principle of these concretions.[5]

We should note further that Whitehead's is *a cosmological philosophy* based upon an aesthetic picture of relations. It is not simply that his *Process and Reality* is called *An Essay in Cosmology;* it is that "Cosmology, since it is the outcome of the highest generality of speculation, is the critic of all speculation inferior to itself in generality."[6] Cosmology as aesthetic vision is, however, the feature of Whitehead's work that must be stressed, for this is the clue to the most direct comprehension of Whitehead's philosophy.

I

"Any author is easy," said William James (in an essay on "Hegel and His Method"), "if you can catch the centre of his vision."[7] The center of Whitehead's vision is to be found in the *picture* of relations that is everywhere present in his work. For example, he once described an event ("a nexus of actual occasions, inter-related in some determinate fashion in one extensive quantum") by picturing a pool of water, and a child tossing pebbles into it.[8] Wavelets, radiating in widening circles toward the edge of the pool, would spring from each splash of a pebble. Where the wavelets from one splash would intersect with those radiating from another an "event" would occur. The cosmos as a field of "actual occasions" is like that, only we should have to suppose the child tossing handful after handful of pebbles into the water, and the intersections occurring innumerably over the surface of the pool (throughout the universe). Each event is an actual entity on its own account; at the same time the momenta of force (the wavelets) are *moving through* each brief occasion and on toward other concretions.

This example of the pebbles in the pool is not singular and incidental, but rather it is typical—indeed, *implicit*—in Whitehead's "envisagement" of things. Thus "the whole spatial universe is a field of force, . . . a field of incessant activity. . . . The modern point of view is expressed in terms of energy, activity, and the vibratory differentiations of space-time. Any local agitation shakes the whole universe."[9] We are led to "a conception of the world as an *interplay* [italics mine] of functional activity whereby each concrete individual thing arises from its determinate relativity to the settled world of other concrete individuals."[10]

What this leads to is the *pars pro toto* principle, or the microcosm-macrocosm relation, or Pascal's view of the universe as "an infinite sphere whose center is everywhere and whose circumference is nowhere." "Thus the continuum is present in each actual entity, and each actual entity pervades the continuum.[11] . . . Each unit is a microcosm representing in itself the entire all-inclusive universe."[12] The best statement, however, is the following: "My theory involves the entire abandonment of the notion that simple location is the primary way in which things are involved in space-time. In a certain sense, everything is everywhere at all times. For every location involves an aspect of itself in every other location. Thus every spatio-temporal standpoint mirrors the world."[13]

Now it is "pretty obvious," as Wallace Stevens remarked of this passage, that these "words [are] from a level where everything is poetic."[14] Whitehead's vision is essentially *aesthetic*—which is one reason, doubtless, why Wallace Stevens through his poetry is a more faithful expositor of Alfred North Whitehead than are most of his official commentators. "Philosophy is akin to poetry," Whitehead concludes in this discussion of the modes of thought; and it is also mystical: "For mysticism is direct insight into depths as yet unspoken."[15] Philosophy begins in wonder; it is not a science.[16] "My own belief is that at present the most fruitful, because the most neglected, starting point is that section of value-theory which we term aesthetics."[17] This would appear to subordinate aesthetics to axiological categories. That this is not the case will appear. But it is the zone within which Whitehead's interest in feeling, appetition, satisfaction, freshness, novelty, adventure, concern, zest, imagination, and the like arise. All these relate to his "category of the Ultimate." They are central rather than peripheral to his point of view (his "speculative philosophy"). They relate to his interest in symbolism,[18] and to his recognition of the existential primacy of expression: "Expression is the one fundamental sacrament. It is the outward and visible sign of an inward and spiritual grace."[19]

This doctrine, so central to Whitehead's speculative philosophy, must be stressed in three further directions. First, it supplants the supremacy of "logic," which tends to hypostatize its subject-predicate forms and to exhibit metaphysics in tautological and abstractive patterns. Aesthetics is wider in scope than logic, and so contains it. "Indeed," wrote Whitehead, "when the topic of aesthetics has been sufficiently explored, it is doubtful whether there will be anything left for discussion."[20]

But more than this, the mode of the process itself is aesthetic;[21] which means that Whitehead's "envisagement" of things is more nearly akin to Heraclitus than it is to Aristotle. To be sure, the Heraclitean vision is modified by the problematic of the *Timaeus;* nevertheless, the "elucidation of meaning involved in the phrase 'all things flow,' is one chief task of metaphysics."[22] The Heraclitean maxim that God and man live each other's death, die each other's life, as well as the central symbols of fire, fountain, lyre, bow, etc., as they appear and function in Heraclitus' aesthetic vision, are speculative philosophy of the Whitehead type. It is the notion of creative advance in Whitehead that makes the difference. With this principle included, the basic "envisagement" of Whitehead's philosophy comes clear: "The ultimate metaphysical principle is the advance from disjunction to conjunction, creating a novel entity other than the entities given in disjunction."[23] Which is almost precisely what Coleridge set forth as the inner nature of poetic creativity in his *Biographia Literaria.*

Now, Professor Christian has very properly called attention to Whitehead's categories of existence and his categories of explanation (with the question about "sorts" and the suggestion about "rules" for the systematic use of the aforesaid categories). But the point that we must take here is that both of these sets of categories must be pushed back up against that which *precedes* them in Whitehead's scheme: namely, the category of the Ultimate. What we find here is that *three* ultimate notions are involved: the "one," the "many," and "creativity." This is, once again, Whitehead's philosophical purview in its categoreal nutshell—triadic, though non-Hegelian, with creativity playing the starring role. " 'Creativity' is the universal of universals characterizing ultimate matter of fact. It is the ultimate principle by which the many, which are the universe disjunctively, become the one actual occasion, which is the universe conjunctively."[24] It might be urged that sec. VI of Professor Christian's paper serves just this purpose: the purpose, that is, of backing up the secondary categories of Whitehead's scheme into the categories of the Ultimate. I would not dissent from this; but, once again, it is precisely here that the primacy of the aesthetic becomes plain, for, from the standpoint of the categories, God is the principle of concretion,[25] and from the standpoint of action, he is at once "the poet of the world"[26] and "the Eros of the universe."[27]

II

I have spoken of the primacy of the aesthetic vision in Whitehead at length because it is, curiously, the dimension of Whitehead's speculative philosophy that is either subordinated or ignored by so many Whiteheadian enthusiasts today, and especially by those who seek his philosophic offices for the doing of theology; and because, also, it seems to me that this is the dimension which does not come clear in Professor Christian's careful and impressive ground-clearing for theology's adjunctive appropriation of Whitehead's work to its own purposes. Professor Christian assumes that both metaphysics and theology have a logical basis, and rules out the possibility that theology may be a productive art, as poetry is. But this is precisely Whitehead's view: that *both* metaphysics *and* theology have an aesthetic base, not a logical one. Professor Christian assumes that *because* metaphysics and theology have a "logical" base, interaction between them is possible; but "interaction," although employed by Whitehead in certain contexts, is not the characteristic metaphor for *this* relation. It is a static expression. One must observe in Whitehead such terms as "interplay," "fusion," "transition," "routes" of creative advance, etc., to capture the way in which metaphysical relations must be grasped. Professor Christian's own metaphorical uses suggest a similar anaesthetizing of Whitehead's vitalistic and dynamic feeling essential to the interplay of things. The stress on "connections" and "interconnections" suggests abstractive, formalistic structuring. The suggestion that the process of living is "like the weaving of a web of many strands" deletes the *movement through* dimension of the pool image. To say that life, or the process, is "like music" is far better, provided we do not think of music in terms of mathematical notations. For here again the "music" occurs, not in terms of a note or a chord sounded in its isolation from the whole, but rather in the *movement through* the aesthetic intention of the passage in the tonal drama of its processive advance into novelty. Or again, when Professor Christian commends Whitehead's speculative philosophy for theological uses *because* it bears a family resemblance to those great systems in the history of Western civilization, this is precisely why Whitehead would *not* be useful: because his work is presented in analogy with those systems of the "static Absolute" from which he has striven so assiduously to separate himself.

Nevertheless, Professor Christian is certainly correct to insist on the grand scheme and the splendid scope of Whitehead's work.

Certainly there is a "rationalism" and a demand for logical judgment and coherence that exhibits Whitehead's speculative genius
in a most spectacular way. Yet it is again, as always in Whitehead, the dipolar problematic of the "one" and the "many" re-
solving its formal obtuseness through the dynamic outcomes of
the creative advance.

Perhaps this is what Professor Christian's argument intends.
For does he not say quite plainly that the discovery of categories
is for the sake of illuminating our prespeculative experience, and
they are not intended to supplant our commonsense view of
things? But once again, when he suggests that the basic question
of speculative ontology is, What sorts of things are there? and
proposes that this question comes close to the "root" of metaphysical thinking, do we not have to remind ourselves of Spinoza's warning that more basic than the "root" is the *soil* out
of which the root comes,[28] as well as of Heidegger's attempt
to retrieve for the Western consciousness a "fundamental ontology" by going behind the tradition of Western "metaphysics"
through reawakening the primary question as to why there is
anything at all. Abstract speculation for Whitehead is for the
purpose of *transcending* the systems;[29] and "Logic, conceived
as an adequate analysis of the advance of thought, is a fake."[30]
Professor Christian, I suspect, would not deny this. My question
is whether he would affirm its opposite: recognize, that is, the
Whiteheadian primacy of aesthetics over logic—for his own language, in this essay, does not seem to carry this awareness. Whitehead puts it bluntly: "Logicians are not called in to advise
artists."[31]

III

What is true of the relation between aesthetics and logic is
true to even a higher degree of the relation between "metaphysics" and theology. To reapply a happy simile of Whitehead's,
there is Aaron's rod, and there are the magicians' serpents: the
only question for theology is which swallows which? If the

metaphysical system is given formal primacy, then the theologian
quite properly objects that something has been left out (just as
the aesthetic is relegated to the status of ornamentation if the
theoretical sciences are given priority over the practical sciences).
If "metaphysics" is used in its traditional manner, theology is
swallowed, which is what contemporary theology has been resisting in all its existentialist forms. But it would appear that Whitehead is resisting it too if he is permitted to come forward on his
own terms: that is to say, in terms of the aesthetic. For the aesthetic requires the factuality of feeling as indispensable to actual
entities, and it requires the metaphorical language of appetition,
feeling, satisfaction, life. Whitehead's terminological innovations
are predominantly descriptive: events, occasions, concretions, etc.

Professor Christian quite correctly brings forward Whitehead's
view of God as the crucial test as to the availability of Whitehead's thinking for the uses of theology. Here again Whitehead
leaves us in no doubt as to the way in which he envisages God.

God is the measure of the aesthetic consistency of the
world. . . . The metaphysical doctrine, here expounded
(in contrast with Kant's rejection of the argument from the
cosmos), finds the foundations of the world in the aesthetic
experience, rather than . . . in the cognitive and conceptive
experience. All order is therefore aesthetic order, and the
moral order is merely certain aspects of aesthetic order.
The actual world is the outcome of the aesthetic order, and
the aesthetic order is derived from the immanence of God.[32]

Professor Christian's summary of the several components of
God's nature is excellent within the limits imposed—his aim,
his primordial and his consequent nature (though the latter
is not specified directly), and his immanent function as the lure
of feeling toward novel forms of being, together with the things
which differentiate this view from that of Plato. I would note
merely the following:

The Whiteheadian view restores to theology the relevance of
the cosmological setting. Theology cannot avoid being effected
by the radical shift in the cosmological presuppositions implicit

in the metaphorical dimensions of its own thought forms. The program of demythologization is one evidence of this effect on the negative side; but it is probably naïve to suppose that theology can construe its own *positive* meanings without filling the void left by the recession of the static forms of the world picture. Here it is misleading to conclude, it would appear, that "the problem posed by Whitehead's philosophy is similar to the problems posed by Neoplatonism in the fifth century and Aristotelianism in the thirteenth century." If our emphasis above is correct, the problems it poses (philosophically at least) are precisely *un*like the historic models, for it insists that the models of the static Absolute, or the *deus ex machina* (in whatever form), cannot be accommodated to the contemporary world picture. This includes "the Semitic God," to which Whitehead frequently alludes. This Semitic or Biblical view, in combination with Aristotle's view of God as the "unmoved mover," produced "the doctrine of an aboriginal, eminently real, transcendent creator, at whose fiat the world came into being, and whose imposed will it obeys, [which] is the fallacy which has infused tragedy into the histories of Christianity and of Mahometanism."[33]

The Whiteheadian view is immanentalist, God being the creative element that supervenes from within the cosmic process to effect the emergence of novel entities. By the same token it is incarnational and historical. By reason of its aesthetic form its cosmology is composable toward the cosmological "story";[34] but is the cosmological story composable toward the eschatological event? To put it another way, can the Whiteheadian event become (in Kierkegaardian language) a moment of absolute significance? Can it sum up and recapitulate the moral drama of the immanent creative enterprise in such a way as that "the acts of God" may climax in a singular event in history, that which becomes paradigmatic and purgative for the moral opposites of joy and sorrow, good and evil, as well as for disjunction and conjunction, flux and durability, freedom and necessity, "God and the World"? Can the lure of feeling endure suffering unto death at the point (the event) where all the opposites collide and exhibit the ultimate novelty of creative reconciliations through redemptive love?[35]

Whitehead's aesthetic sense is predominately Hellenic. It is the image of harmony that presides over his thinking, rather than the moral earnestness of the covenantal imagery of the Hebraic God-consciousness.

It is possible that aesthetics in Whitehead's sense might be qualified by this Hebraic consciousness: which might be an instructive project, for the fact that the Hebraic imagery has not, in its turn, been qualified aesthetically has always carried it toward literalism and/or moralism, which, in traditional systems, infiltrates Christian doctrine destructively.

> Protestant theology [Whitehead advised some three decades ago] should develop as its foundation an interpretation of the Universe which grasps its unity amid its many diversities. The interpretation to be achieved is a reconciliation of seeming incompatibilities.[36]

The last sentence moves us in the right direction, but a direction in which the incompatibilities are not "seeming," but real, and the local event derives its reconciling (and thereby, creative) outcomes by petitioning the "Lamb slain from the foundation of the world."[37]

A concretion of concretions would seem to be existentially implicit (though perhaps not "necessary") in an immanentalist aesthetic world view such as that of Whitehead. Is its occurrence vitiated by the fact that both God and the world, in this view, "are in the grip of the ultimate metaphysical ground, the creative advance into novelty"? Ethically, and perhaps cosmically, it is understandable that both God and the world are the instruments of novelty each for the other (God and man die each other's life, etc.). But is the ethical dimension "fubbed" (as Wallace Stevens would say) by the form of the antecedent metaphysical commitment?

Christianity, Whitehead has said, is the religion in search of a metaphysic. But is the metaphysic of Christianity already implicit in its action, and is it therefore the only religion for which the metaphysical structures of philosophy and the world-building of science are authentically symbolic?—and therefore already dispensed with (as being structurally tied in formulate fixations to that which is perishing, that which, in the Kingdom, is already creatively surpassed)? Is this the mystery that Nietzsche grappled with, which immanentalism cannot express, and which historical theology (in its logicometaphysical alliances) has always misunderstood?

On another level of problematic, is Eden (to which Whitehead refers) the primordial function of God that is always in the course of being lost (the mystery of perishing), and original sin the temptation to inhibit the creative advance through coercion of the emergent forms, whether rationally or willfully (instead of learning the knack of complying with the lure of feeling—of letting grace happen)? All authentic creativity has its roots in "the Unconscious." Does Whitehead's aesthetic view remain rationalistic in spite of himself by reason of its dependence upon a classical psychology? And must theology suffer the same fatality if doctrinally constrained by the same curtailment?

Are the criteria appropriate to an organismic aesthetic ontology—whether in art, philosophy, theology, or politics—the criteria of taste, adequacy, teleological and dramatic coherence, and satisfaction? Was T. E. Hulme therefore correct in holding that what is needed today is a *Critique of Satisfaction* beyond Dilthey's proposal of a *Critique of Historical Reason*?

Is there a radical void, or vacuum, at the core of Whitehead's dipolar, triadic movement toward creative advance? The problem of nothingness (which Whitehead notes in Plato, but does not resolve), of naughting, of no-thinging would seem to be essential to the transitional phase of the movement from perishing to becoming, if becoming is to be a creative advance rather than an atomic rearrangement or emergent succession.

Does not Whitehead's view of the logos as expression require a doctrine of silence? Does it lean toward Heidegger here, or toward Nishida's philosophy of nothingness, or toward Zen, rather than toward Christianity? Or should we say that in Whitehead the revision of our ways of seeing is so radical that we cannot properly be Christian without ceasing to be "Christian" in the traditional modes of thinking and saying? *Creatio ex nihilo* at last becomes central here in that the living novel occasion is born out of the no-thinging of the old.

These, along with many others, are questions that must be answered *in re* the question of theology and the "new metaphysics." Formally, it would appear that the interplay of the new metaphysics and theology would move toward a theology of symbolic forms; Biblically, it prefers the Johannine Logos theology. It sees grace as the experienced mode of the "divine persuasion," the theology of the Kingdom as the consequent form of the nature of God; existentially, it places one always at the point where ethically and cosmically the extremes meet in the persistent movement of disclosure, reconciliation, and creative advance—the teleological aim at satisfaction. Philosophy, as Whitehead says, "may not neglect the multifariousness of the world—the fairies dance, and Christ is nailed to the cross."[38] Can theology do less? Perhaps *this* is the question posed for theologians by "speculative philosophy." Or conversely, does the event of Christ's being nailed to the cross belong to "the multifariousness of the world" in the same sense (with due allowance for "gradations of relevance") as the event of fairies dancing? Is this perhaps the question posed by theology for speculative philosophers?

NOTES

1. *Process and Reality*, p. 16.
2. *Ibid.*, p. 16.
3. Alfred North Whitehead, *Modes of Thought* (Capricorn Books, G. P. Putnam's Sons, 1958), p. 112.
4. Cf. Alfred North Whitehead, *Science and the Modern World* (A Mentor Book, The New American Library of World Literature, Inc., 1949), pp. 155–157.

5. *Ibid.*, p. 174.

6. Cf. Alfred North Whitehead, *The Function of Reason* (Beacon Press, Inc., 1958), pp. 86–87.

7. William James, *A Pluralistic Universe* (Longmans, Green & Co., Inc., 1943), pp. 86–87.

8. In a lecture in the course "Cosmologies, Ancient and Modern," which it was my privilege to attend at Harvard University in 1930–1931. *Process and Reality* was the text! The definition of "event" is from *Process and Reality*, p. 113.

9. *Modes of Thought*, pp. 186, 188.

10. Alfred North Whitehead, *Symbolism: Its Meaning and Effect* (Capricorn Books, G. P. Putnam's Sons, 1959), p. 29.

11. *Process and Reality*, p. 105; cf. *Symbolism: Its Meaning and Effect*, p. 39.

12. *Religion in the Making*, p. 91; cf. also p. 100.

13. *Science and the Modern World*, p. 99.

14. Wallace Stevens, *Opus Posthumous*, ed. by Samuel French Morse (Alfred A. Knopf, Inc., 1957), p. 192.

15. *Modes of Thought*, p. 237; cf. p. 68; if it is the task of philosophy to "rationalize" mysticism, coordinating its insights by "novel verbal characterizations" (!).

16. *Ibid.*, p. 232; Alfred North Whitehead, *Essays in Science and Philosophy* (Philosophical Library, Inc., 1947), p. 113.

17. *Essays in Science and Philosophy*, p. 129.

18. *Symbolism: Its Meaning and Effect*, p. 62.

19. *Religion in the Making*, p. 131; cf. p. 137.

20. *Modes of Thought*, p. 86.

21. *Ibid.*, p. 231.

22. *Process and Reality*, p. 317; note also p. 43.

23. *Ibid.*, p. 32.

24. *Ibid.*, p. 31.

25. *Science and the Modern World*, p. 174.

26. *Process and Reality*, p. 526.

27. *Adventures of Ideas*, p. 326.

28. "Rooted in," means, in Whiteheadian terms, "participating in the formative process."

29. Cf. *The Function of Reason*, p. 76.
30. *Essays in Science and Philosophy*, p. 96.
31. *Adventures of Ideas*, p. 336.
32. *Religion in the Making*, pp. 99, 104–105.
33. *Process and Reality*, p. 519.
34. Cf. *ibid.*, p. 254.
35. Cf. ibid., p. 531.
36. *Ibid.*, pp. 217–218.
37. *Ibid.*, p. 529.
38. *Ibid.*, p. 513.

III B

THEOLOGY AND METAPHYSICS

Shirley C. Guthrie, Jr.

There was a time when theologians could enter immediately into conversation with philosophers about God and the world. It might be a friendly or hostile conversation, but it was taken for granted that a conversation was both possible and worthwhile. But now in a "world come of age," the era of the "secular man," a theologian must answer some preliminary questions before the topic "theology and metaphysics" can seem either possible or worth the trouble.

First, he must decide whether "God talk" is still theologically possible. If he decides that as a theologian he can no longer talk meaningfully about God, he can only refuse to talk with the philosopher at all, or decide that although theology cannot talk meaningfully about God, perhaps philosophy can—in which case the conversation becomes not one about the relationship between theology and metaphysics, but simply a philosophical discussion. I want to take the position that we *can* as theologians talk about God, because, in Professor Christian's words, we have a given starting point for our thought in a particular historical event—in the life, death, and resurrection of Christ. Whether or not we can do it adequately and relevantly, we must at least attempt to develop Christian theology, as he says, from its own roots: the assertion that God has revealed himself in Jesus Christ as we know him in the Bible. We cannot make such an assertion and talk about it as glibly as we could a few years ago. The absence and hiddenness of God have become more a reality for us than his self-revelation. We are so confused by the conflicting claims about the metaphysical and mythological Jesus, the old and new historical Jesus, the kerygmatic and the existential Jesus, Jesus the "New Being" and Jesus the "Word of God," that we are no longer sure what we mean when we say "Jesus Christ." The Bible has perhaps become a closed book for us, so that we can no longer depend on neat systems of Old and New Testament theologies. We do not know how to communicate to a secular world what little we do think we know. But nevertheless, we cannot give up trying to talk about God—*this* God. "Theology and metaphysics" is therefore a *possible* topic.

But even assuming that in however a confused and inadequate way we *can* as theologians talk about God with philosophers— *should* we? Is it worth the trouble? What would we have accomplished if we solved the problem of the relationship and distinction between the meaning of the word "God" in theology and in metaphysics?

Suppose there were a metaphysics which could convincingly argue that God is logically necessary to explain the world. Suppose it could show how he both transcends and is immanent in the world; how the world depends on him, yet is real and free in itself. Suppose, further, that it could be shown that this metaphysical system which reasons from the world to God and back again is surprisingly similar to the conclusions of a Christian theology which claims to reason in the opposite direction. Suppose, in other words, that despite the differences in their approach to the one whole truth, we could with hard work achieve at least a fruitful coexistence if not a marriage between theology and metaphysics. And suppose, finally, we devised a language to communicate all this.

Would the word "God" then regain its meaning in the modern world? Would faith in God become possible again for secular men (including the secular man in us theologians)? Would there be restored a sense of the reality of God, which we theologians ourselves lose and cannot communicate so long as we try to think in terms of a theology of revelation alone? Would lives in the world become more meaningful, and could we with our new metaphysical-theological language enable others to find more meaning in their lives in the world?

I think the answer to all these questions is a clear *no*. And it seems to me that the theologians who speak for the secular man in the world come of age, *and*, surprisingly or perhaps not so surprisingly, the theologians who speak for a Biblical way of looking at things are one in telling us why. Neither the modern secular man nor the Biblically-oriented man lives in terms of metaphysical-cosmological problems and answers (although metaphysical and cosmological presuppositions may be consciously or unconsciously in the background). If they find it at all, they find the reality by which they live not above the world, or behind the world, or in an all-embracing world view, but *in* the world itself—the pragmatic world of political history and social change and everyday human life. The realm of metaphysical speculation is too "religious" for both. Modern secular man lives without God in the world. The Biblically-oriented man believes in God and interprets his own life and the history of the world in the light of God, because he believes that God "acts" in the world. But both are world- and history-oriented.

Before we can decide that a metaphysical-theological discussion would be profitable, in other words, we have to come to terms with the impressive arguments against such a conversation from such diverse thinkers as D. Bonhoeffer, Paul Lehmann, Paul van Buren, and Harvey Cox. In Cox's *The Secular City*, for example, he argues that "the metaphysical deity survives only in those quarters where vestiges of the classical ontologies hold out, where the stream of secularization has temporarily been escaped"[1]—among preachers, theologians, philosophers, religious people, and among an increasingly smaller number of academically trained people in the humanities who represent a "residue of Christendom." If we are to speak of God relevantly to the vast majority of modern men, we must, Cox says, "place ourselves at those points where the restoring, reconciling activity of God is occurring, where the proper relationship between man and man is appearing."[2] Speaking of God must therefore be political:

> It must be a word about people's own lives—their children, their jobs, their hopes or disappointments. It must be a word to the bewildering crises within which our personal troubles arise—a word which builds peace in a nuclear world, which contributes to justice in an age stalked by hunger, which hastens the day of freedom in a society stifled by segregation. If the word is not a word which arises from a concrete involvement of the speaker in these realities, then it is not a Word of God at all but empty twaddle.[3]

I think Cox and those who argue as he does are right. Not as we become involved with old or new metaphysics that talk abstractly of God and the world, but only as we become involved in the concrete human issues of our time, and only as we translate the meaning of God's revelation in Christ into political-ethical terms—only then will we learn ourselves and communicate what we are talking about when we say "God," and when we say "God was in Christ." It seems to me that in our time a "theology that develops from its own roots" must be a political-ethical theology, both because only such a theology will make sense to modern secular men, and because only such a theology looks for God and talks about him where he gives himself to be known.

All conversation between theology and metaphysics, then, seems to be at best a waste of time and at worst a self-destructive enterprise for theology.

The trouble is, we cannot evade ontological questions simply by saying that we will work and think and speak in a political-historical, not in a metaphysical, framework. Cox says: God is "not to be identified with some particular quality in man or in human reciprocity, and he is not just a confused mode of speaking about relationships between men."[4] "He is able to be present in a situation without identifying with it."[5] In other words, God is both transcendent and immanent in the world. The reality of God and the reality of the world, God and man, are related but not identical. But how are we to think of these relations and distinctions? We can of course refuse to ask such a question, but if we do, how are we to avoid *either* making "God" a fancy way of talking about man (in which case, it would be better to drop "God talk" as unnecessary), *or* presupposing without recognizing it the old "metaphysical deity" of what Whitehead calls "unreflective supernaturalism"? Will not all our talk about "what God is doing in the world" become superficial and unconvincing?

This line of thought leads me to agree with what I understand to be Professor Christian's main argument: theology is not metaphysics, but theology cannot do without metaphysics. Everything depends, in my judgment, on maintaining the proper *order* of thought in relating them. If theology develops "from its own roots," as Professor Christian suggests it should, then we cannot *begin* with ontological questions or a metaphysical system, and make "what God is doing in the world" conform to and confirm the possibilities and necessities of a given ontology. We have to begin with the political-historical activity of God interpreted in the light of the historical events in which Christian theology roots. We have to try to understand who God *is* in terms of what he *does*. To begin in such a way admittedly involves beginning with some conscious or unconscious metaphysical presuppositions, but everything depends on the theologian's not giving those presuppositions a *programatic, determinative* significance, and his being willing to let them be changed and corrected by what he learns from the sources and framework of his own discipline. *Conscious, deliberate* ontological thinking has its place logically *after* theology discovers and talks about God in his political activity. Metaphysics is necessary to theology, in other words, but it can only be an instrument, not a dictator. By this I do *not* mean that a dictatorial, absolute metaphysics is to be replaced by a dictatorial, absolute theology. Theology is also a limited human enterprise that cannot master but only serve the truth, and it must constantly submit itself to correction by the truth. I *do* mean that according to what Professor Christian calls the "logical basis" of theology, there is a given *priority* and *se-*

quence in theology that cannot be reversed: first, the historical-political and *then* the ontological-metaphysical.

If we decide that we cannot simply choose between theology and metaphysics, the question then becomes: What kind of metaphysics? Without being an expert on Whitehead, it seems to me that his metaphysics offers itself as a very promising candidate just because in contrast to traditional metaphysics it does not force us to choose between history and ontology, but attempts to take both into account in their interrelationship. Whitehead's metaphysics includes the same two elements that I believe responsible Christian theology must include: God's being in terms of his action in the world, his action in the world as an expression of his being. Could it be that the Christian theologian and the Whiteheadian metaphysician are two blind men feeling the same elephant? Is it the same whole truth they are getting at from their different points of view? If this is possible, and I think it is, then whichever one is feeling the head of the elephant would do well to listen to whichever one is feeling the rear end, and vice versa.

What can Christian theology learn from Whitehead? I want to mention two things which I find implicit in Professor Christian's paper and explicit in his book on Whitehead.

1. Whitehead's metaphysics can expose and therefore free Christian theology from its dependence on other metaphysical systems. Even when it knows better theoretically, Christian theology still has a tendency unconsciously to identify or confuse the truth it tries to understand and communicate with Platonism or Aristotelianism or Stoicism. And when it criticizes the theological thinking of others, it tends to be involved in the conflict of one metaphysics with another rather than in a genuine theological conflict. This is in any case a danger in my Reformed tradition, whether or not it is true of other traditions. So, for instance, when we speak of God as "infinite, eternal, and unchangeable," we have a tendency to think of the attributes of an unmoved mover rather than of those of a living God. When we think of the "world," we have a tendency to think of something

like Plato's or Aristotle's world rather than either of the Biblical creation or of the modern universe. Whether or not Whitehead's new metaphysics can help us in a theological way to talk about God correctly and meaningfully, he does expose the impossibility of a theological retreat to past metaphysical systems. He can free us from even an unconscious dependence on them, and free us to look for alternative solutions.

2. I say the same thing in another way when I suggest, secondly, that Whitehead's criticism of "traditional theology" can remind Christian theology to take seriously what it should have learned—and at its best has learned—from its own sources. He can force us consistently and rationally to develop what we already know as theologians, and perhaps give us some tools to do so. He criticizes traditional theology for three things: for its unreflective supernaturalism, its assumption that God is unaffected by the world, and its assumption that God is the sole determiner of the world.[6] All three criticisms are valid. But Christian theology does not have to turn to Whitehead to learn that God is not an arbitrary power related to the world only as a *deus ex machina*, that what happens in the world makes a difference to God, that "new things" can happen, that God's unchangeableness is not static but creative. Contemporary theology learned all this by self-criticism in the light of its own sources. But partly because we are so steeped in classical metaphysics, and partly because by its very nature theology tends to think of the reality of God at the expense of the reality of the world, we easily forget what we have learned. If we pay attention to Whitehead, we will not be able to forget. Perhaps we shall find that as theology tends to lose or to treat too lightly the world, in the last analysis Whitehead tends to lose both the radical transcendence and the radical immanence of God. But if we think we have to say something more and different, we cannot do it at the cost of his insistence on the reality and freedom of the world—not without denying our own best insights. From our own logical basis, we can only try to do better, not less, than he has tried to do from his logical basis; that is, take seriously and speak con-

sistently about the reality and freedom of God *and* the reality and freedom of the world in their interrelationship.

Professor Christian concludes his paper by saying that "Christian theology must develop from its own roots, but its life may be *fertilized* and *invigorated* by influences [such as Whitehead's philosophy] that penetrate the soil in which it grows." I have argued that both from a Biblical and from a secular point of view we must try to formulate a theology in terms of nonmetaphysical, political-ethical categories which may be called to order and saved from superficiality and irresponsibility by Whitehead's metaphysics. If I understand Professor Christian correctly, I think we are in substantial agreement.

He does not say *how* this "fertilizing and invigorating" or "calling to order" can be accomplished. Without letting Whiteheadian categories be determinative or thematic, could they be used *along with* nonmetaphysical categories and language to clarify and contribute to the translation of Christian truth into political-ethical theology? Could theologians concerned to make such a translation learn from Whitehead what is to be learned there and devise ways of expressing it accurately, but in such a way that people are not forced to become Whiteheadian metaphysicians before they can understand and talk about the Christian faith?

A theology that roots in a historical event in which it is claimed that God encounters us in a man, and which therefore expresses itself in terms of "what God is doing in the world to make and to keep human life human" (Paul Lehmann) will inevitably sound hopelessly "mythological" to the philosopher. In my opinion, theology need not be overly concerned about that. What we do need to be concerned about is how we "mythological" theologians can use what we learn from the metaphysical philosopher and at the same time stick to our own particular task. Perhaps we shall have made some progress if we can agree *that* this is a legitimate task resulting from a promising confrontation between theology and the new metaphysics, even though we cannot yet spell out the *how*.

NOTES

1. Harvey Cox, *The Secular City* (The Macmillan Company, 1965), p. 246.

2. *Ibid.*, p. 256.

3. *Ibid.*

4. *Ibid.*, p. 260.

5. *Ibid.*, p. 261.

6. William A. Christian, *An Interpretation of Whitehead's Metaphysics*, pp. 383 ff.

IV

SOCIAL SCIENCE AND

THEOLOGY

Talcott Parsons

I

To me the relation of social science to theology is a very interesting topic. Indeed, the future of theology is very much involved with it. And for a social scientist who has, like myself, been rather considerably concerned with the relations of religion and society, the relation of his professional discipline to the discipline of theology, which is the intellectual wing of religion, if one can say so, presents some very important problems.

I would like to approach this topic in a rather broad historical context, and start with a very general observation, namely, that among all the great historic religions Christianity probably has been most distinguished by its readiness and capacity to integrate its religious point of view with the great developments of secular culture in relation to which it has stood. This feature of Christianity goes back to the very early phases and, despite all the vicissitudes which have been undoubtedly complicated and sometimes full of conflict and tension, nevertheless the main trend has persisted right through Christian history.

We are all very much aware of the fundamental importance of Greek philosophy in the shaping of Christian theology in the relatively early church. Without Neoplatonism or some functional equivalent, there would probably have been no Christian theology as we know it. This development continued through the involvement of Augustine with classical philosophy, and, of course, in the medieval phase of the Western church culminated with Thomas Aquinas, with his basic concern with the rational aspect of theology and the services that the philosophy of Aristotle could perform in shaping it.

The story has then continued into another great phase, different from the predominantly philosophical one, which opened with the advent of modern science, modern in a very broad sense. We know that there have been many conflicts between science and religion. The church, the Inquisition, condemned Galileo, and there were a good many other episodes of that sort. But the bigger picture is the fact that Christian thought and Christian theology in particular have come to be specifically integrated with the developments of modern science. In the case of American Protestantism, I think very particularly of the importance of the science of Newton and the philosophy of John Locke for the theology of Jonathan Edwards, who was perhaps the greatest theologian in American history so far, certainly in Protestant American history. The late Perry Miller is the authority for the statement that Edwards understood Newton and Locke at a level far superior to that of most of the professional philosophers of his day, to say nothing of the more orthodox theologians of his time.[1] We are also familiar with the chapter of the relation of Darwinism to theology and the furor that focused about that a century ago, recalled by celebration of the centenary of the publication of *The Origin of Species* only a few years ago.[2] I suggest that a *new* chapter in this relation of theology, and specifically of Christian theology, to the secular-scientific disciplines has opened broadly in the last century and has been rapidly developing in our own generation with the emergence of the social sciences, which is my particular topic.

Before entering upon it I may suggest that if one looks at the history of the relations of theology and secular thought in a broad perspective, it becomes fairly clear that there is a very interesting ambivalence in the attitude of religious thinkers, including both technical theologians and a broader religious-intellectual public, toward the developments of secular-empirical thought with which religion has had to relate and come to terms. Very schematically I would like to suggest two aspects of this attitude, and that they tend to appear in temporal sequence. We need not go back to the philosophical cases that I mentioned, and we can restrict attention to those concerns which seem to emerge when new understanding is achieved of the empirical order of the world in which man is placed. The initial impact on religion of great intellectual advances is to generate a strong tendency for the reaction to be one of dismay and often eventually hostility, but this initial impact is usually followed by assimilation and understanding.

This was true for the early Copernican revolution. On the one hand, by displacing the planet earth from any possible position as center of the physical universe, by implication it certainly derogated the position of man. If man's terrestial home is only one planet among many, as it had certainly begun to appear, from the Copernican point of view, our sun is only one of many suns in the universe. Then what is man as the special creation of God, created in his image, as the most important part of the total creation? This was a very serious question. And we know the incredible developments of celestial mechanics since the Copernican days, and how very, very tiny a part of the physical universe the planet earth is now known to be—I say, not thought to be, but known to be.

We can take a similar point of view with respect to Darwinism and its bearing on the doctrine of special creation. Man, after all, is an animal, and it is very easy to go from there to the suggestion that he is *only* an animal, just like any other animal. In this connection it is easy to ignore the fact that man is the product of an incredibly long and complicated process of evolution, even looking at it in the purely biological framework, and therefore is not just an amoeba or something like that, but a very special part of the organic world. His specialness is not derogated by the theory of organic evolution but, rather, emphasized by it.

II

The impingement of these scientific movements on the traditional religious views of the human condition generated serious
conflicts, with eventually relatively full resolution of them. But
starting in a really serious way about a century ago, roughly con-
temporaneous with Darwin, there began to be another very important intellectual movement with even more radical implications.
Man, that is, came to be seen not only as a biological animal but
as an actor in the field of social relationships. He, in his presumptively more or less rational behavior in pursuing his ideals or his
interests, relates to his fellowmen and thereby *creates* a deterministic order. The development of economics, reaching a certain cul-
mination in the theories of Marx, has gradually borne in upon us
the fact that the interrelationships generated by human action itself
in social systems are highly deterministic.[3] In other words, as a
member of a system of social relationships, interacting with his
fellows, man is, as the individual man, not specifically free to do
anything he wants. In fact, the initial impact of this insight has
tended to be the idea that he becomes a slave of his own interests,
whether it be as the wage slave, or as the slave of capitalistic exploitation, or the "profit slave" of the Marxian picture of the businessman. The true Marxian picture of the businessman, the capi-
talist, is not that of a "bad" man who, through his ill will, is doing
injury to his fellowmen just because he is a sinful, cussed sort of
character, but that of one who is caught in a *system*, by virtue of
which he either has to exploit his fellowman or go under. There
is no alternative, unless the *system* is revolutionized.

This is a determinism almost with the pathos of predestination.
People are caught. But as individuals they cannot change their
situation. But what are they caught in? Simply the consequences
of deciding to do what they want to do, of following their own
interests. This is a rather terrific point of view. I do not at all
subscribe to the Marxian version of it. I think that in Marxism the
determinism of the so-called capitalistic system was vastly over-
exaggerated. And Marxism comprised a very narrow, limited analy-

sis of the forces at work. But it has had the impact of emphasizing determinism. Furthermore, it did not emphasize the other side of the picture, which is not simply the "other side of the coin," namely, the fact that social organization, through the economic division of labor, is also liberating. It opens opportunities for doing things, for gratifying interests that could not possibly be opened on the basis of a primitive economy. The fantasy of the virtues of primitive communism in Marx's theory is egalitarian all right, no doubt about that, but it is equality in abysmal poverty. And incidentally, the whole Marxian point of view strongly emphasizes the virtue of the productivity of the so-called capitalistic economy.

I do not want to dwell on Marx's views, but simply to cite them as probably the most important first stage of a movement that by virtue of its deterministic emphasis has developed much further since Marx. A second chapter, coming along not very long after, was that associated with depth psychology, specifically Freudian psychoanalysis. The central point is that here is another set of features of the human condition, this time the personality of the human individual, where "deterministic" order deeply limits human freedom. The key concept, I think, is that of the unconscious. In view of the development of the structure of thought about human behavior as of that time, it was very natural for this to run off in the direction of the interpretation that what really stands back of the unconscious is biological instinct.[4] It clearly turns out, however, not to be nearly as simple as that, since the internalized objects and values of society are also deeply involved. Unquestionably, however, not merely at the external level of economic conditions, but also in the depths of his own personality, man is not as free as he has fantasied himself to be. Evidence of this insight is the argument that is going on intensively to this day, as to whether the person who commits an outrageously criminal act does so because he has deliberately decided to violate the order of human society or because, being psychologically sick, he can not help himself. Most people who are familiar with this area, social workers, criminologists, psychiatrists, etc., would quite agree that there is no simple solution of this problem. Man is not simply subjectively-psychologically the captain of his fate. When he sins, he does not do so only in rebellion against what he knows to be right. He does so in large part because he cannot help it. The relation of this problem to the Christian tradition of helplessness is patent, but is *only* sinful human nature to blame?

Now, I think that sociology in our own time has gone even farther. There is a sense in which *its* determinism is a kind of synthesis of economic determinism and psychological determinism. Looked at on one level, in one set of respects, this derives from the fact that the social order is seen to be, as the technical term goes, internalized in the personality of individuals. From one point of view, the result is to draw the deterministic circle apparently even tighter and to make it more inescapable than it would be from either of the others, the economic or the psychological perspective taken alone.

It seems reasonable to think that among a great many intellectuals of our time, the prevalence of the theme of alienation and the fear of overconformity, etc., which is so prevalent, is probably not understandable without the impact of these new conceptions of determinism which are the product—ideologically distorted of course, but nevertheless the product—of genuine advances in the understanding of human behavior.[5]

This is, I think, generally the initial impact. It takes a lot longer, and it takes greater intellectual sophistication, as well as what you might call emotional adjustment, to understand that this new knowledge, and the determinate conceptions of order which it formulates, are the foundations of new and greater freedoms. With respect to the physical world, this is perfectly obvious to us today. Leaving out the impact of astrophysics, without scientific knowledge of the physical world, what kind of technology would we have? It is quite clear that technology does not contravene the order of nature; it *utilizes* it. Without scientific knowledge of organic life, where would medicine and public health be? The application of scientific knowledge in those areas has simply transformed the conditions of human life.

Thus, to look at it in personal terms, I am in my sixties. If I had lived a little more than a century ago, I would be one of very much less than 50 percent of my age cohort who had lived beyond the early thirties. Taking being born alive as the reference point, in a little over a century the normal span of human life has been more than doubled. Is anyone to say that this is a derogation of basic human values? And how has it happened? It has happened by understanding the order of organic nature and utilizing that understanding. I think the same basic principles are coming to a head in a situation of substantially greater pathos in the field of the psychosocial order.

The problem can be posed, again with a physical illustration, as follows: Obviously, man has only a very minor role in the precipitation of moisture from the atmosphere, in its flow down mountain and hill side and river valleys. The "order" of these processes is objectively given and "constrains" him, but if man is shrewd enough to build a dam at a strategic point in the river valley, he can generate electric power from the fall of that water. This is a very fine thing, but may not seem to be anything very special because the water would have flowed into the sea anyway. Man is just intercepting it at a strategic point and running it through a generator instead of the unmodified riverbed. You don't go so terribly much farther when you say, to take one of the simpler cases from medicine, if man simply intercepts the typhoid bacillus and prevents it from entering the body by controlling water and milk supplies, and therefore people don't die of the typhoid, well, he isn't intervening in the order of nature much. I mean, who's going to stand up for the right of typhoid bacilli to kill people? It would take a very extreme Buddhist in the tradition of the ahimsa doctrine to say that typhoid bacilli should have priority over human life. This, however, is, as we know in certain religions, a real problem.

But, there is an immense difference when we deal with the social order, deriving from the fact that the human social order is *man-made* in a sense in which man's physical organism is not man-made. It is made by motivated human action, and this is the crucial thing, and I would use the word "order" advisedly. It is an "order," not simply an agglomeration of arbitrary acts of will. It is much more, and this is what the social scientists are talking about. They are trying to understand the elements of order, the interdependence which originates in acts of will, and which form the conditions in which further acts of will can take place, and for better or worse do take place. These, however, become intermeshed with each other, in such ways as to produce ineluctable consequences of human beings acting the way they do, deciding the way they can be expected to decide, and relating to each other in the way they can be expected to relate to each other.

Such structures of order are not the kinds of things that operate only on the level of gross economic competition and things of that sort, but extend almost into the innermost depths of the individual personality. We can be said to be, as persons, what God made us, but we are *also* what our experiences in our families make us, and our parents were just as human and just as imperfect as we became as parents and adults of the next generation. They are not gods, and human beings who have been formed by their experience and interaction in the family *cannot* behave as if they had never been brought up in families. They are not totally free agents. I am not saying that they are not in any sense free agents. Of course they are, but they are not totally free agents. And they are partially unfree agents not only because they are limited by physical exigencies, but also because they are limited by the exigencies of their own social character and that of the others with whom they have to live. This is a very deep-going determinism.

But there is not the slightest doubt about the fact that this so-cial organization or order is, *at the same time*, the essential ground of the great freedoms of a great modern society.[6] I do not want to overestimate the modern, but certain aspects of the liberating character of social organization have become far more evident in the modern age than they were before. We have a tendency to dwell on the pathologies and distressing aspects of our own time. I mentioned the fact that human beings live, on the average, sub-stantially more than twice as long in the so-called "developed" countries than they did a century ago. This is no mean liberation, simply because the man who dies at thirty-five is not going to be free to do the things he might have done between thirty-five and seventy. To say that he is freer dying at thirty-five than if he had lived in good health to be twice as old is a very hard statement to accept if it implies that in some ways it was a freer society when people died on the average at thirty-five. Note, the expectancy of life at birth in our society is now almost exactly seventy years. This is an extraordinary fact, in spite of wars, and rumors of wars, in spite of gang delinquency, etc., and in spite of automobile accidents. This, the freedom to live out a long life span, is only one of many freedoms that have increased in an unprecedented fashion in our time.

III

Following on the great developments of the integration of Christian theology with philosophy of classical origin, and much later with natural science, I have sketched the impact in the modern world of three intellectual movements in the field dealing with human action, that of economics, with special reference to the Marxian emphasis on economic determinism, that of the psychology of personality, with reference to the internalization of social objects and cultural norms to become constitutive parts of the personality itself, and that of the recent sociological study of social organization and interaction.

Each of these developments of the sciences of human behavior has on the one hand brought to a heightened awareness the sense in which human action is subject to the constraint of a system of order that imposes conditions on the individual which are clearly beyond his personal control. In a modern society even the humblest of us is dependent on its wage and price structures. We cannot simply shape to our desires the remuneration for our services through employment or the prices of the goods we buy; we must accept the going rates of the labor and consumers' markets. Since our personalities have been formed in our life experience within our families and then among our peers and in the course of our schooling, we cannot suddenly as individual adults decide to become quite different kinds of personalities; our personal "fates" have been largely determined. Sociology then gives us an understanding of the many ways in which we are bound together in interdependence in our social relationships, far more broadly than through the marketplace. We *must*, both by the force of external sanctions and interdependence and by our own characters, conform broadly with the imperatives of our social organization, with its rules and norms, as a fundamental condition of the maintenance of the social order that makes the higher orders of human life possible at all.

There is, however, as we have noted, another side. It is already clearly visible at the level of organic life. The higher organisms are characterized by more elaborate differentiation and hence organization than the lower ones. This organization can work effectively only if the parts are subjected to definite controls. But, under definable conditions, these same highly organized species are the ones which have developed the greatest capacity to cope adaptively with the conditions of their environments. Through organization they have acquired quite new levels of freedom of action.

This keynote is vastly extended at the human cultural and social levels of organization. It is visibly and conspicuously extended not merely to the analogue of a species, i.e., a total society, but to individuals and various orders of subgroups. We have come to understand that, at the deepest levels, the freedom and capacity of the individual does not stand *over against* collective organization and cultural tradition, but is most intimately involved with it; it is a function and product of that organization, though under certain conditions it can be, and of course is, blocked by specific forms of organization.

This general thesis is illustrated in the three contexts I have sketchily outlined. It is completely understood in economic science, including its Marxian wing, that through the division of labor and organization of production far more can be produced than in primitive economy. More can be produced through markets and monetary exchange, and the factors of production can be mobilized from far wider sources, giving managers of productive organization far greater freedom. The ultimate consumer also gains enormously in freedom, in that he has a larger "real income" than otherwise, and through the market mechanisms he has freedom of choice of items to buy, of sources from which to secure them, and freedom in suiting his own time in making or postponing his purchases. The constraints imposed on both producers and consumers by economic organization therefore constitute in certain respects the underlying conditions of a range of freedom for both categories which without them would be impossible. We can say that modern economics has taught us to understand quite precisely how these two aspects of the human economic condition are related to each other.[7]

The same basic principles obtain in the relation between the determinism of development of the individual personality through life experience in addition to hereditary constitution, and capacities for free and responsible action. The most obvious context in which to point this out is in the cognitive field, which in turn relates to technical skills. The learning by the individual, first, of language, and then through language, as well as observation and supervised experience, of already known fact and theory about the world is of course at the very least a tremendous shortcut compared with learning "the hard way" without benefitting from the contributions of others. Beyond that, however, we know that it is strictly impossible for the totally isolated individual to reach anything approaching a "cultural" level of knowledge and skill unaided. An excellent example is language itself, which is always culturally given, and only modified in minor respects by single individuals—even great literary figures—though the cumulative effect of millions of such modifications may transform a cultural system.[8]

The knowledge and skill learned in the course of social experience is an obvious set of conditions for the capacities to move about freely, to avoid danger, to cope with many features of the environment, and to take advantage of opportunities. The level of generalization of knowledge which we call science confers by far the highest levels of freedom on man. But not only is science a recognition of the determinate elements of order in the world of objects of its study, but at the same time it is inherently a *social* phenomenon. It must be learned by the individual in relation to a socially borne and developing tradition in the context of social organization and institutions.

More generally the new freedoms that are given by personality development through "social learning" or "socialization" are the consequence of learning to participate (including communicate) with others in an organized cultural and social system. Making certain parts of the structure of this system parts of the individual's own personality of course constrains him, but it is the most fundamental individual condition of his possible freedom as a mature human being.

The last of the three contexts I have outlined, that of the development of sociology itself, constitutes both a generalization and a synthesis of these other two. It rests on the understanding that the deterministic element of the motivation of the individual goes far deeper into the personality than the utilitarian individualists, whose philosophy underlay the development of economics, realized. At the same time it involves the understanding that the elements of deterministic order at the social level are by no means restricted to the level of economic interdependence and power relations, but extend to a broad range of factors of solidarity, consensus, and conformity which affects most aspects of ordinary life.[9] The same basis of insight, however, which has brought understanding of this determinism, has gradually brought us to understand the liberating possibilities of organization and integration on these levels. There is no space to develop these themes here, but I may note that a complex national community in which diverse ethnic and religious groups not merely coexist but come to be positively integrated is dependent on a system of order that prevents certain types of particular interests, e.g., in exploiting ethnic or religious prejudice, from gaining full expression.

All these considerations bring me closer to the central theme of this discussion, namely, the relation between theology and the social sciences. As one last empirical point, I may suggest that the development of the present level of theoretical insight in economics, the psychology of personality, and sociology is basically connected with a major development in the sociocultural system itself. This is, on a new level of a very old evolutionary sequence, the institutionalization of the pursuit and transmission of knowledge itself and the entrusting of this function to a professional group working within a distinctive organizational framework. This, essentially, is the modern academic or university system. Its institutionalization in cultural terms first required the clear establishment of the difference between the secular intellectual disciplines and theology, as the cognitively predominant branch of the formulation of religious positions. As distinct, the pursuit of the secular disciplines then had to become autonomous from—which is not the same thing as dissociated from—theology. All this crystallized in the main American academic system only in the last third of the last century.

Then the system of the secular disciplines themselves had to become differentiated and elaborated. The older humanities have been the primary base, but they have been extended to comprise both the natural and the social sciences, so that the three groups taken together now constitute the main cognitive universe of the academic system, with theology retaining an essential, but also in some respects problematical, position.

This secular system of disciplines could not have become consolidated without the development of the social sciences and the clarification of their position.[10] It is in them that the basic cultural tension between determinism and freedom comes to a focus. The tendency of the natural sciences to be interpreted in the pattern of determinism is very clear—they have tended to formulate elements of order in the humanly significant world which were emphasized as being given independently of human interests or wishes. Gradually, as seen above all in the case of the biological sciences, the problems of synthesis became unavoidable. What of the "behavioral autonomy" of higher organisms relative to their environments?

The humanities, on the other hand, could for long simply be treated as concerned with the recording and "understanding" (in the German sense of *Verstehen*) of the creations of the human personality. Some elements of determinism, as in those of "historical" association and sequence, have been present from the beginning and became increasingly salient. Thus an important cultural figure "could not" have made the contribution he did, had his predecessors not laid the groundwork—without the Sophists and Socrates, how make Plato's work intelligible? Conversely, once certain "ideas" had been promulgated, how could subsequent cultural events be understood without referring to them?

Generally speaking, the humanities have been very strongly focused on linguistic expression, and it is perhaps in the understanding of language itself that the relevant problem of determinism has become most salient. Clearly, the users of a language, even the most "creative" among them, did not "start from scratch" but utilized a "framework" or a "code," the main outline of which was ready-made for them. Insight into this situation favored pushing back the locus of creativity to something like the "genius" of a "people," e.g., the Greeks, who are somehow held to have created the language of its great cultural contributions. If this conception is to be more than the virtual tautology that "Greek was created by the Greeks," its basis is in need of considerable clarification. Within such frameworks, however, the general tenor of the humanities has been to conceive human action as a "creative" process, as one in which the freely taken decisions of individual human beings have brought about fateful consequences for humanity as a whole. Indeed, this is one basis on which "humanism" has gotten into trouble with the religious traditions at a number of points.

The very rise of the social sciences has, however, driven the general problem to a newly acute level of tension and, many have held, inevitable conflict. As I have suggested, to the determinism of the physical world and of organic life there has been added a whole series of economic, psychological, and social determinisms, so that in the pressure to "conformity" the last vestiges of human freedom have seemed to many to disappear. (There is a special romanticism in the allegation that this situation is peculiar to *modern society,* and that in the "good old days" of simple societies the individual was basically "free." What is new in our day is the *understanding* of social order, not the fact of its existence.)

In sum, we live in a society of which two things must be said. First, because of the very extension and complexity of its organization, new and often very mysterious constraints are continually being imposed on previously defined spheres of freedom of action—e.g., when someone behaves unacceptably, you cannot now simply proceed to treat him as willfully at fault and punish him, but you must consider the possibility that he is "mentally ill" and "can't help it"; hence, it would be unjust to punish him. At the same time, however, ours is a society in which the cognitive understanding of these dilemmas has not only become imperative, but procedures for promoting it have become institutionalized. The development of university systems in the field of the secular cognitive disciplines is no mere accident of recent times, but is deeply grounded in the cultural imperative of our traditions. In particular, the inclusion of the social sciences in an increasingly prominent place is a centrally important phenomenon. On the one hand, there is a basic public recognition of the seriousness of the problems posed. On the other, there is a vote of "confidence" in the possible rationality of coping with them by sanctioning the activities of a professional group, a group whose role is that of devoting available cultural resources to their understanding and to the application of this understanding to practical affairs.

IV

Theologians will immediately recognize the relevance of the conceptual structure of the above argument to their own great traditions. The apparent dilemma of freedom and determinism, of course, roots in dual facts: First, it is assumed that a totally sovereign transcendent God created the universe without any reference to finite human concerns. Man as part of the creation is obviously to be regarded as subject to whatever patterns of order were divinely ordained, and the idea of *any* human autonomy in these respects would, at first sight, appear to be nonsensical.

Secondly, however, God is said to have created man "in his own image," which is to say as an active entity, capable of *doing* things in some sense on his own initiative and responsibility. As such, man is entrusted with a mission to do God's will, which eventually evolved into the conception of establishing the divinely "planned" human society on this earth which, though a "Kingdom of God," might be said to be "governed" by men. The responsible agent of the divine plan cannot very well at the same time be treated as having no sphere of autonomy whatever, but as being only a "creature" of an indefinite range of factors and conditions mostly beyond his understanding, but certainly beyond his control.

This second basic theme of Christian theology makes man himself not only part of the creation subject to the divinely ordained order but also within his own sphere a creative agent. And, above all, it was as a member of a social community that he has functioned as a creative agent. This theme, of course, goes far back. It is distinctive, in our tradition, to the early people of Israel, who were conceived as a social collectivity, covenanted with each other and with Yahweh, and given a special mission, a divinely ordained mission in the world. Then with the first phase of Christianity this concept of mission, a collective mission—I want to emphasize the collective—was given to the church of Christ. The church in its early stages was a mere enclave, a little Christian island in a pagan sea. Men were to live in the world but not of it. The injunction was to render unto Caesar the things that were Caesar's. Caesar, however, was not a Christian prince but was a pagan emperor of a pagan society. In fact, it was not expected that there would be any human society after the imminently anticipated Second Coming.

But as Christianity became adjusted to expecting the permanence of life in this world, not for any given individual, but for the succession of generations, then it began to shape the idea that Ernst

Troeltsch has so classically stated of the possibility of a Christian society. And Troeltsch classically outlined how medieval Catholicism presented the first version of the idea of a Christian society.[11] It was a very qualified version, one dependent upon a series of gradations of religious commitment and merit, from the religious orders at the top through the church to the various graded orders of secular society. But even the humblest Christian layman was not simply a pagan. He was included, in a qualified sense, in this great collectivity of Christendom. His status was defined by this heritage.

Now, the movement from this graded system to a more unequivocally specifically religiously oriented social collectivity is a crucial aspect of Protestantism, especially what Weber called its "ascetic" branch.[12] There are many different phases that could be followed through. I can distinguish only two. First was the Calvinistic version of the earlier phase that was very sharply institutionalized in early New England. This was a presumptively Christian society in which the elect not only governed but constituted the church itself; there was no nonsense then about religious freedom or toleration. They threw Anne Hutchinson out and hanged some Quakers, etc. It was a grimly established church with the presumptive elect the sole members of the church, but with the holding of the reprobate majority to the discipline of the church. It was a pretty grim society. I am glad that I did not live then. But a great idea, unquestionably, it was. It was the idea classically put, I think, by Perry Miller in his various works, e.g., *Errand Into the Wilderness*, of really establishing a holy community, a Kingdom of God on earth.[13]

Now, the direction of development which this society took was a liberalizing direction that, with the basic principle of voluntarism established, led to a second version. It was no longer a society in which the predestined elect acted as self-appointed and perhaps somewhat dubiously, divinely appointed, and presumed to rule over the others and to exclude those who did not meet their standards. The movement was, on the contrary, toward the conception of the church as a voluntary association, the access to which was open to all who would confess the faith and really devote themselves to it, which meant access to salvation and to all goods of the church and membership in the church. The voluntary principle went along with the principle of pluralism. Religious toleration came to be accepted as a matter of course, and with it, denominational pluralism. There was no longer one church. There were an indefinite number of churches. Now, this became the unique American institution, unique for its time, of separation of church and state.[14]

This eventuated in a broad pattern which has been institutionalized in the general social community of Western democracy. For important reasons, though, it has developed more fully in this country than elsewhere. The result has been, in a special sense, a "secular" society, which institutionalizes political democracy, and a certain fundamental equality of the status of citizenship; of course, we've been going through a particularly acutely difficult new phase of that inclusion process, with respect to race relations in our own time, and the end is a long way off. But the direction seems to me to be pretty clear. Various types of individualism have appeared, but within the frame of the conception of a good society. And by no means least important, this society, which started out as basically a Protestant society, which only tolerated non-Protestants, has in our own time achieved the inclusiveness of an ecumenical Judeo-Christian society.[15] The election of John F. Kennedy to the Presidency as the first Roman Catholic President of the United States and, almost more, the extraordinary ritual significance of the reaction to his assassination as not merely a nationwide, but an international, reaction has put the symbolic seal on the fact that this is no longer in the old sense a Protestant nation, but an ecumenical nation.

These are only a few of the barest highlights of the religious constitution of the new modern version of the "Christian society." By most of the standards of our dominant tradition of liberal Protestantism, it is a society that must be said to have advanced far along the road of institutionalizing the basic moral precepts of its religious base, however far it falls short of the desired level of perfection. We all know the seriousness of the inequalities and injustices that remain, of the failure to control the use of violence adequately, in particular to insure against the occurrence of war, and the like. Perhaps most serious of all is the fact that the Western world of predominantly Christian background has achieved so much higher a level of social welfare for its populations than so much of the rest of the world—how is this situation to be equalized?

V

This though highly qualified, still very striking success of the (especially) Protestant Christian mission for this world presents very acute problems in terms of the religious tradition itself, because of the background of insistence on the fundamental qualitative difference between all things spiritual and things temporal, and hence the tension between them. To hold the "Secular City," to refer to Harvey Cox, to be in any direct way related to the "City of God" seems to many to be wholly sacrilegious.[16] And yet, if it is the realization of the divine plan, however imperfectly worked out, it must be in some sense "sanctified." In this very deep dilemma, perhaps one symbolic reference of the "God is dead" formula might be that the "Old Man," having completed his "job" so far as mankind is concerned, might as well die, since he is scarcely needed anymore.

The clear distinctness of social science vis-à-vis theology must be insisted upon. But social science is of prime importance to the theologian because clarity about what has in fact happened can most effectively be made available to the theologian through the kind of understanding of the society we live in which the social sciences have contributed. In this sense it may be held that the contributions of Troeltsch and Max Weber have sunk far more deeply into our definitions of the modern situation than most are aware of, and these definitions in turn are related to a far more ramified system of social science knowledge, extending as I have suggested in economic and psychological as well as sociological directions.

My own analysis has started from the fact that theology is an *intellectual* discipline, the child of the marriage of Christian faith with the great cognitive traditions of the classical world. Unquestionably, this intimate relationship was inherently a part of the close connection between religion and society which is involved in the wordly mission of man in the whole Judeo-Christian tradition. That religious tradition has been the most important *single* agent—though one of many—in the development, in the Western world, of what we call *modern* society.

The autonomous—relative to religious tutelage—secular society is the outcome of this historic process. But equally, the autonomous —relative to theology—secular intellectual disciplines are the cultural outcome of what in essentials has been the same basic process. Sinçe the religion and society problem is so crucial to the whole religious interest of our time, and since our religion has given a special position in its long tradition to cognitive understanding of its problems, it can hardly fail to be the case that specialization of cognitive effort and competence in the understanding of society assumes a special place in the relations between theology and secular learning.

It would seem to follow that the social sciences must soon in some sense assume the position, among the secular discipline groups, which has, in relation to theology, been historically occupied by the humanities. It is here that "spirit" (almost in the German sense of *Geist*) and "world" with its connotations even of the physical world, most intimately meet. For theologians to center their worldly cognitive attention only on the humanities is too easy, since they are basically "religious" anyway. To be completely preoccupied with their relation to natural science on the other hand bypasses the critical "human" problems. It is in the social sciences that the intellectual battles concerning the meaning of the relation between the ordered "creation" which is independent of man, his interests, and his will and the process of "creative action" in which man is the divinely appointed responsible agent will have to be worked out.

NOTES

1. Cf. Perry Miller, *Jonathan Edwards* (Meridian Books, Inc., 1959).

2. Sol Tax, ed., *Evolution After Darwin*, 3 vols. (The University of Chicago Press, 1960).

3. A. D. Lindsay, *Karl Marx's Capital: An Introductory Essay* (London: Oxford University Press, 1947).

4. Lionel Trilling, *Freud and the Crisis of Our Culture* (Beacon Press, Inc., 1955).

5. Cf. Winston White, *Beyond Conformity* (The Free Press of Glencoe, Inc., 1961), for a delineation of the negative reaction to this knowledge among intellectuals.

6. Cf. Freud's famous dictum, "Where Id was, there Ego shall be."

7. Cf. Paul A. Samuelson, *Economics: An Introductory Analysis* (6th ed., McGraw-Hill Book Company, Inc., 1964).

8. Sigmund Freud, *The Ego and the Id* (London: Hogarth Press, Ltd., 1927), and Bärbel Inhelder and Jean Piaget, *The Growth of Logical Thinking from Childhood to Adolescence* (Basic Books, Inc., 1958).

9. Emile Durkheim, *The Division of Labor in Society* (The Free Press of Glencoe, Inc., 1949).

10. Talcott Parsons, "Unity and Diversity in the Modern Intellectual Disciplines: The Role of the Social Sciences," in *Daedalus*, Winter, 1965.

11. Ernst Troeltsch, *The Social Teaching of the Christian Churches*, tr. by Olive Wyon; with an introduction by H. Richard Niebuhr, 2 vols. (Harper Torchbooks, The Cloister Library, 1960).

12. Max Weber, *The Protestant Ethic and the Spirit of Capitalism*, tr. by Talcott Parsons (Charles Scribner's Sons, 1958).

13. Perry Miller, *Orthodoxy in Massachusetts, 1630–1650* (Beacon Press, Inc., 1959) and *Errand Into the Wilderness* (Harper Torchbooks, 1964).

14. Paul A. Freund and Robert Ulich, *Religion and the Public Schools: The Legal Issue, the Educational Issue* (Harvard University Press, 1965).

15. Will Herberg, *Protestant—Catholic—Jew* (Doubleday & Company, Inc., 1955).

16. Cox, *The Secular City.*

IV A

SOCIAL SCIENCE AND

BIBLICAL PERSPECTIVES ON MAN

Walter Harrelson

Professor Parsons has served us well. He has provided broad perspectives within which to view past and current relations between social science and theology. He has rightly underscored the increasing importance of the social sciences for theology as over against the humanities, pointing out that many of the issues in contemporary theology are greatly clarified by the knowledge and understandings developed by social scientists.

I have but a single point to make. In my judgment, Professor Parsons has not given sufficient attention to the contributions of ancient Israelite understandings of God, man, and the world, and to the adoption and elaboration of these contributions in early Christian thinking. My desire is by no means to insist that ancient worthies anticipated contemporary social science. It is, rather, to indicate that Biblical faith is a great deal more compatible with contemporary understandings of man's social existence than had been believed in past centuries. These observations are presented not primarily as a critical note to the paper of Professor Parsons but rather as an expansion of his historical sketch and a forecast of what seems to me certain to be an even more fruitful partnership between social science and theology in coming years.

The Biblical World View

Ancient Israel, or some of its spokesmen at least, sketched a picture of man's place in the world that was strikingly different from the prevailing picture in the ancient Near East. In the Bible we have a picture of a world created by God at the "beginning" of the temporal process. This world was no emanation from the divine realm. It did not depend upon renewal through cultic acts. It was held in existence by its Creator, but the Creator worked upon it from a position of nearness to it. He appeared in the world that he had made, without ever being contained in any of the materials or persons through which or whom he was manifest. Indeed, the ancient Israelites had very little to say about God's being, his essence. They knew him through his earthly appearings. Nor did they know much about the heavens. Theirs was an earth-bound faith. Either they made sense of their lives by reference to God's activities in the world of which they were a part, or they had no alternative but despair. The models or archetypes characteristic of ancient peoples were used very sparingly by ancient Israelites. An earthly happening or object was not referred to its archetype in the heavens in order for it to be understood. God the Creator had brought into being a world that was not divine. He appeared in the midst of that world of his creating, revealing to men the meaning of their lives and the operations of their world.

Man's place in this world was conceived as located at the apex of all created things. Man was charged to exercise mastery over the world, acting under God's overarching sovereignty. Man was not merely free to investigate the world, to come to terms with its mysterious operations. He was required to do so, for otherwise he could not exercise proper sovereignty over it. Spokesmen for ancient Israel went very far toward desacralizing the world. It was a most worldly world that they lived in, ruled by God, brought into existence by God, directed toward the consummation of God's purposes for it, but nonetheless a creature subject to the direction of God's special creature, man.

Of the greatest importance was the Israelites' recognition that the world did not begin with Israel. God created not Israelite man at the beginning, but man, male and female. The story of Israel's beginnings comes later on. God's choice of Israel was centrally important, but Israel was not the first people on earth. This, too, is without analogy in the ancient Near Eastern world, to my knowledge. The ancient Israelites viewed the work of God in creating mankind to govern the world as an act of God not vested in some special people, some churchly group, endowed with special revelation. All men, male and female, in virtue of their humanity, are charged to bear their part of the work of the Creator. They are to rule over the world under God's sovereignty, seeking to discover what makes for life and peace and blessing, and prodding the earth to be more productive for the good of all creatures, human and nonhuman.

The same desacralization of the world shows itself throughout the Bible. The Israelites were strictly enjoined against using the power of the divine name as a weapon against their enemies. They were denied any full explanation of the name "Yahweh," since to know the inner meaning of the name would (by ancient view) put one in a position to evoke the powers resident in the name for one's own uses. They were not permitted to make images of other gods, of course, but neither could they make images of Yahweh. It was not possible to find in the created, nondivine world any adequate representation of its Creator. Nor was it possible sufficiently to know God to be able to fashion any suitable image of him.

This is a religion that can only be designated agnostic, in terms of ancient theologies. Ancient Israel had less knowledge of the workings of the divine than did any of her neighbors.

The story of Israel's receiving human kings to lead her is also told in a thoroughly secular way. God indeed agrees to the anointing of Saul and David as Israel's first kings. But kingship in the ancient world was "lowered from heaven." This institution was recognized widely to confer upon its incumbents divine or near-divine status. Not so in Israel, or at least, not so in the accounts given of the kingship. Rather, we have a picture of human beings being elevated to this position after a long period of Israelite history during which there were no kings. Israel consisted, sociologically, of twelve tribes, all descendants of a certain

Jacob. That is itself a remarkable secularization of the rise of a people.

Israel's great Temple in Jerusalem was erected late in her history, with God's approval, but built by a foreign architect at the site of a pagan cult center. The community did not require a temple in the years before its building, and the community survived when the Temple fell in 586 B.C. But in the ancient world a god without a temple was hardly worth man's attention.

Israel's great prophets took sharp stands against the incursion of foreign elements into the community's worship. Yahweh alone was God, and the people could not worship both Yahweh and Baal—so Elijah (I Kings, ch. 18). But the prophets borrowed extensively from the religious ideas and practices of their neighbors. They used the stuff of ancient Near Eastern religious literature to shape their understanding of Yahweh's governance of the world, Yahweh's purpose for his people. Israelite religion can indeed be called syncretistic, if the term be used in a broad sense, for the shapers of Israelite religion borrowed on all sides from religious notions. They demythologized them, to a very large extent. They brought the fundamental meanings of ancient Near Eastern society into connection with the concrete details of Israel's history and the history of the nations. The marriage of the high god with his divine consort, which was the archetype of all fecundity in the natural world, became an image of Yahweh's marriage with his people Israel, through the act of covenant-making. The cultic activities and symbols fed upon the narratives of Israel's past history.

Within the Israelite community, special knowledge normally reserved to the priests became the property of the entire community. In no ancient Near Eastern community outside of Israel would the priests have laid before the community the most precious secrets of their cultus, but the Pentateuch is replete with catalogues of such secret information, exposed to all the community.

Moreover, the Israelite community could survive the loss of its most precious cultic objects, the interruption of its most central ritual acts. The world did not depend for its continuance upon the dramatic re-presentation of the myths of creation or other myths accounting for man's place and activities in the world. The Kingship, the Temple, the Ark of the Covenant, the sacrificial system—all these could disappear, and the faith of Israel remain. It should not surprise us, therefore, that a Jewish teacher in the first Christian century, whom we Christians identify as the Christ, could attack the Sabbath, fasting, and other elements of the Jewish cultus, or that subsequently the Christian community should continue to identify itself as inseparably related to Judaism while opening its membership to Jew and Gentile alike.

My point is a simple one, but of some importance, I believe. The orientation toward the world found in Biblical literature is astonishingly nonreligious, in the customary sense of that term. Biblical spokesmen, or many of them at least, spent most of their energies in attempting to summon their communities to discern the mysterious workings of God within the ordinary world, workings of God that aimed at peace and well-being for all men, that also summoned men and women to labor for the realization of his purposes for them and for the world. While the world depended upon its Creator, Guide, and Redeemer, God's creature man had been summoned to come to terms with this world and to serve in company with God to realize the divine objectives for God's world.

The Bible and Man's Freedom

The picture sketched by Professor Parsons of man's freedom in the midst of a determined social order also has its counterpart in Biblical literature. Biblical man understood himself to be free to rebel against God's purposes and be destroyed, or freely to conform his life with those purposes and to reap the fruit of obedience. In the ancient Near Eastern world, man generally understood himself to be subject to any and every kind of action by the powers, divine and demonic, that surrounded him. Israelite and Christian man understood himself to be subject to the inexorable demands of the one God, demands that could be understood, could be generally recognized to be for man's good, and which if spurned, brought not freedom and new delights, but ruin.

The Biblical presentation of man's place in a created world, open toward a future as yet unknown, provided and still provides a dynamism for man's social existence. Man's freedom is circumscribed by the world, God's creation, and by God's demands laid upon men to fulfill the destiny awaiting them. It is not circumscribed, however, in the way in which human freedom in the ancient Near Eastern world was limited. For to recognize man's place in the world, and to be summoned to accept and to deal creatively with the possibilities open within that world of God's creation—this was to be charged to do just what social scientists, as I understand them, suggest that men must do. Determinism is no threat to freedom; it is the ground from which true freedom springs. Surely this is what the doctrine of divine providence was intended to affirm.

Cooperation Between Social Science and Theology

Professor Parsons has indicated what social science can contribute to theology. His is a responsible and illuminating statement. It is entirely unobjectionable, in my judgment. Already the various disciplines of the social sciences are of critical value to the theologian, and I suspect that they may already have become more important than the humanities.

Theology also has some contributions to make to the social sciences. These it can make without in any sense seeking to invoke claims of special knowledge, special demands for a commitment to a particular form of religious faith. These latter are not to be despised, but the contributions of theology to social science do not depend upon them.

1. Theology can assist social science in the determination of the character of a religious community or tradition, help to identify its special contributions to the life and culture of a people. We need not depend alone upon the methodologies of anthropology and sociology to determine the place and character of religion within a society, invaluable as those methodologies are. And the social scientist need not be suspicious of theological

methods that are used to delineate the religious dimension of a given culture or period, although he has a perfect right to insist that the methods used be sound and subject to critical controls.

2. Theology can and must provide guides, along with other disciplines, for the making of decisions, for the use of the freedom men have to reshape their world. Such guides need not be put by theologians only in the terms familiar from their tradition. New and fresh ways of providing such guidance must be sought. A simple guide that means much to me is to suggest that that action is good which enhances rather than damages man's life in community. Here the realism, the secularity of much Biblical literature comes into the picture. A secular picture of responsible social existence is not likely to differ greatly from one that is Christian or Jewish.

3. The most important element that theology can contribute to social science is, I believe, its presentation of the necessity and the means for acts of celebration. A society is not whole unless it provide means for celebration, for ecstatic response to the goods and meanings of life. The disciplines of social science can take account of this human need. Professor Parsons' own work gives ample place for it. Theology does not engage in such acts of celebration; it does point to their critical importance and seeks to indicate how, in changing cultural circumstances, men and women may affirm the joys and sorrows, the goods and the ills of life through responsible acts of celebration.

And it may be that precisely in such acts of celebration man is able to transcend, for the moment, the gap "between the ordered 'creation' which is independent of man, . . . and the process of 'creative action' in which man is the divinely appointed responsible agent." Theology and social science must both take account of the import of men's participation, through such acts of celebration, in the depths and heights of the world they know. Here theology has the task of holding up for attention the dimension of mystery, of depth, which if lost sight of, can make man's life and labors tepid and tasteless.

QUESTIONS TO
TALCOTT PARSONS

Oliver Read Whitley

Since I have read Professor Parsons' material extensively, and have used it with much appreciation in my teaching of theological students, it is perhaps inevitable that in my remarks I may be reacting indirectly to things that he says elsewhere, but which are, nevertheless, directly related to what he has said in his present address. I shall want to put several questions to Professor Parsons. These questions are designed to provoke discussion of points that I think need further clarification. They do not necessarily mean that in a given case I disagree with his point of view. I simply want further information before I make up my mind.

My questions about Professor Parsons' views on the matter of the relationship of the social sciences and theology arise out of my feeling that he seems to be suggesting a wedding (not necessarily of the "shotgun" type) which will in some sense unite these disciplines. I therefore rise to answer the imperative, "If there be any here who know any reason why these two should not be joined together . . . , speak now." Ultimately, I do not find myself opposing the marriage, but until certain matters are cleared up I would prefer that we hold off announcing the "engagement."

My first question has to do with Professor Parsons' reference to the alienation of the intellectuals. He suggests, correctly, I think, that there is a relationship between the developments in the sciences and that alienation. But I would like some assurance that he is treating that alienation with the seriousness that it deserves. The concern about the impact of the deterministic and positivistic implications of behavioral science models of man is genuine and points to real issues, which I am not sure Parsons sufficiently acknowledges. The question of whether contemporary models of man in the social sciences are unduly deterministic and/or positivistic is far from settled. At times, Professor Parsons appears to be aware of this. For example, in what I consider to be a very important footnote in his stimulating discussion in *Religious Perspectives in College Teaching*, *"In Sociology and Social Psychology,"* he says, "More positive aspects of religion, independent of the strains inherent in the human situation, may be equally important, but are more difficult to get at *in the context of the intellectual traditions of modern social science."* [1] This suggests that the social sciences are better equipped to handle some aspects of human behavior than they are others, and it seems to hint at the possibility that some important dimensions of the human situation may not be adequately dealt with in terms of the intellectual conventions currently entertained in the social sciences. Moreover, Parsons' brilliant account of the "voluntaristic theory of action," as a reaction to the "positivistic theory of action," suggests that in some ways his work might well have taken a somewhat different direction than it has. The theory of action as developed in *The Social System* [2] and elsewhere in his writings might be taken to present man as a *niche* in a system, whose values, attitudes, sentiments, etc., are adequately accounted for in terms of the nature of social and cultural systems. In what sense can we speak meaningfully of freedom in this context? [3]

My second question is, in a sense, an extension of the first one. The question can be stated quite simply. Are social science models in any sense "self-fulfilling prophecies"? Robert K. Merton has developed the notion of the self-fulfilling prophecy as follows. "Public definitions of a situation . . . become an integral part of the situation and thus affect subsequent developments. . . . The self-fulfilling prophecy is, in the beginning, a false definition of the situation evoking a new behavior which makes the originally false conception come true. . . . The misleading rumor create[s] the very conditions of its own fulfillment."[4] Merton was, of course, discussing the question of how false definitions and rumors, if acted on and responded to as true, create the very conditions to which they refer. His specific context was the place of the self-fulfilling prophecy in race relations. Here I want simply to raise what seems to me to be a relevant and cogent question. Is there not a sense in which the kinds of theoretical models used in the social sciences may function as self-fulfilling prophecies? I do not argue that this is necessarily the case, but I think it is a question worth pondering.

My third question has to do with what seems to me to be an undue stress upon the *continuities* between Christianity (particularly in its theology and its value orientations) and what Professor Parsons calls the cognitive culture in the sciences. Does not Parsons need to emphasize the discontinuities between these realms to a greater extent? For example, his account of the development of Western society too easily takes for granted that "the Kingdom of God" idea is synonymous with, or is a derivative or a different version of, the developments he summarizes under the rubrics of "the Protestant ethic," or "the good society."[5] In this connection, I want to raise two points, one deriving from the work of H. Richard Niebuhr on *The Kingdom of God in America,* and the other from Winthrop Hudson's treatment of *The Great Tradition of the American Churches.*

In regard to the idea of the Kingdom of God, Niebuhr points out that this idea "had indeed been the dominant idea in American Christianity . . . but . . . it had not always meant the same thing. In the early period of American life . . . 'kingdom of God' meant 'sovereignty of God'; in the creative period of awakening and revival it meant 'reign of Christ'; and only in the most recent period had it come to mean 'kingdom on earth.' Yet . . . these were not simply three divergent ideas, but . . . they were intimately related to one another, and . . . the idea of the kingdom of God could not be expressed in terms of one of them alone. . . . Kingdom on earth without sovereignty of God and reign of Christ was meaningless."[6] Professor Parsons seems to me to be under the impression that these different meanings of "kingdom of God" are synonymous, and that they can be separated from one another. If this is the case, he has not adequately understood an idea that seems to be essential to his interpretation of the relationship between American society and its religious culture.

Professor Parsons rightly stresses the importance of religious freedom and the traditions of voluntaryism that have developed in our society, as making possible the kind of pluralistic society which most of us understandably value so highly. He does not, however, seem sufficiently aware that the price of this, so far as the American churches are concerned, has been a degree of accommodation to the surrounding culture that has changed the terms on which religion and society are related to each other. He appears to have a deep respect for the fact that the roots of American value orientations are ultimately in the religious aspect of our culture. The question is whether these roots can remain strong under the present degree of accommodation of religion to culture and society generally in America. This is the point Winthrop Hudson has raised when he says that "when churches succumb to the pressures of secular life and fail to exhibit a distinctive quality of faith and life, the separation of church and state . . . loses its point. . . . Ultimately the churches find themselves with little to say that is not already being said by the generality of the community."[7] Apparently, one cannot be as certain as Professor Parsons seems to be, that voluntaryism in matters religious will have desirable effects. "Complete voluntaryism alone is not an automatic guarantee of the health and vitality of the churches. It is only when the coercion of voluntaryism is translated into a compulsion to fulfill a distinctive vocation in society that the churches are enabled to kindle the urgent enthusiasm and wholehearted commitment which is necessary to vigorous institutional life."[8] Along with Parsons, I rejoice in the pluralism of our society, and in the freedom that such a society makes possible. But when the church's accommodation to the culture goes as far as it has in American society, I think that attention must be paid to the problem implied in the statement of Winthrop Hudson. Parsons apparently sees no problem in this accommodation of religion to culture, but surely if the church subculture merely reflects and reinforces the values and norms of the larger culture, theological orientations cannot be said in any significant sense to "inform" that culture.[9]

In the fourth place, Professor Parsons appears to overstress the order side of the freedom-and-order dilemma. He is without doubt correct when he says that freedom depends upon order, in the ways that he suggests it does. Man does gain certain freedoms when he learns to understand the structures that make up the "order" upon which life in this world is based. But should not more emphasis be placed upon the other side of the coin—the possibility that order can become tyrannical, and that it cannot really be defended simply because it is order? I do not want to get involved in the business about functional sociologists inevitably being ideologically conservative, a frequently expressed charge. There is a danger here of unproductive "labeling," a dubious enterprise at best, especially in view of the fact that Professor Parsons' commitments to liberal causes is well known. But he *is* very concerned about the maintenance of systems and structures, and perhaps it is fair to ask whether this does not at least influence his views about the freedom-and-order dilemma, which is so basic to understanding and implementing the concerns of a democratic society. At times, it seems to me that Parsons is somewhat idolatrous of systems and structures.

Finally, I would ask whether, in Professor Parsons' view, theology can do anything for the social sciences. His approach to the problem of the relation of religion to American society seems to indicate that in the proposed marriage only one partner can do something for the other. I am not content merely to treat this as a case of "complementary needs in mate selection." The proposed marriage, if it is to be consummated, might better be of the "colleague" variety. I do not have in mind the extreme version of the situation indicated in William Kolb's proposal that we might, in the interest of more adequate empirical work in the social sciences, substitute Judeo-Christian models of man for deterministic ones.[10] Yet the question whether theology is to be the passive or dependent partner in this marriage, or a fully participating equal colleague, needs further consideration. It is not clear to me that Professor Parsons sees any possibility of dialogue between theology and the social sciences other than a conversation in which the social sciences speak and theology listens, afterward hastening to adapt its views to what the social sciences have stated.

In considering the question of whether theology has anything to contribute to the marriage we have been talking about, I think it is of the utmost importance to look at the doctrine of man that has emerged from the contemporary work of the behavioral and social sciences and ask what its implications may be. For this purpose, the concluding section of Berelson and Steiner's *Human Behavior: An Inventory of the Findings of the Behavioral Sciences* is most illuminating. "How . . . might we characterize the man of the behavioral sciences?" they ask. "He is a creature far removed from his animal origins . . . a creature of enormous plasticity . . . a creature who needs to simplify reality in order to cope with it effectively; a creature subject to the influence of complex 'forces,' whether from the outside or the inside . . . a creature who is subject to the probabilities of influence; to whom everything is natural that he is familiar with, and most other things unnatural."[11] Being the kind of creature suggested in this "portrait," man "lives not only with the reality that confronts him but with the reality he makes."[12] For the behavioral sciences, man is preeminently social in his nature. While the traditional images of man have emphasized reason, faith, impulse, or self-interest as motivating factors, it is the social definition of any or all of these that is stressed in the doctrine of man developed in recent years in the behavioral sciences.

The behavioral science image of man appears to be clear, comprehensive, and in many respects substantial. That being the case, it is somewhat surprising to find Berelson and Steiner acknowledging that a certain richness of human existence has managed to fall through the "screen" of the behavioral sciences.

The inventory of behavioral science findings has, they point out, "little to say about central human concerns: nobility, moral courage, ethical torments, the delicate relation of father and son or of the marriage state, life's way of corrupting innocence, the rightness and wrongness of acts, evil, happiness, love and hate, death, even sex."[13] How is one to account for the fact that so much of real importance about life in this vale of tears has not come within the purview of the behavioral sciences? In this connection, Berelson and Steiner mention the relative "youth" of the social sciences, which might possibly be taken to imply that when these sciences "come of age" they will fill in these crucial gaps in our knowledge about man. More significantly, they refer to "the price paid for method, for system, for abstraction: the concern of science for concepts, for replicability, for objectivity, for rates and patterns."[14] Relevant to this point, they quote Robert S. Morison to this effect: "The scientific method . . . is most successful when it has reduced natural phenomena to 'pointer readings.' Most of what makes life worth living . . . is deliberately circumvented or simply omitted."[15]

The conclusion to which all of this seems to point is quite clear. "Between the image of life that appears in the world of the behavioral sciences and the image in the world of art, there are differences worthy of reflection. Not yet, anyway, do the behavioral sciences see life steadily and see it whole."[16] I am one of those who believe that theology is more akin to art and to literary criticism than it is to metaphysics or science (and here I advance a proposal that is likely to be contested by thinkers of various persuasions) and I would interpret the conclusion reached by Berelson and Steiner as opening the way to a conversation between theology and the social sciences in which theology would not only listen but talk.[17] It might be useful, for example, if the theologians were to continue to remind the social scientists of the dangers inherent in their sometimes unacknowledged tendency to transform theoretical models, heuristic devices, and even root metaphors (such as equilibrium) into metaphysical and/or ontological statements.

NOTES

1. Hoxie N. Fairchild, *et al.*, *Religious Perspectives in College Teaching* (The Ronald Press Company, 1952), p. 297, note 3 (italics mine).

2. Talcott Parsons, *The Social System* (The Free Press of Glencoe, Inc., 1951).

3. On this point, see Dennis Wrong, "The Oversocialized Conception of Man in Modern Sociology," *American Sociological Review*, Vol. XXVI (1961), pp. 183–193; and Talcott Parsons, "Individual Autonomy and Social Pressure: An Answer to Dennis Wrong," *Psychoanalytic Review*, Vol. XLIX, (1962), pp. 70–79.

4. Robert K. Merton, *Social Theory and Social Structure* (The Free Press of Glencoe, Inc., 1957), p. 423.

5. Parsons develops his ideas in this area fully and brilliantly in his contribution to the *Festschrift* for Pitirim A. Sorokin in "Christianity and Modern Industrial Society" Edward A. Tiryakian, ed., *Sociological Theory, Values, and Socio-cultural Change* (The Free Press of Glencoe, Inc., 1963), pp. 33–70.

6. H. Richard Niebuhr, *The Kingdom of God in America* (Willett, Clark & Company, 1937), p. x.

7. Winthrop S. Hudson, *The Great Tradition of the American Churches* (Harper Torchbooks, The Cloister Library, 1963), p. 9.

8. *Ibid.*, p. 10.

9. In this connection, it might be added that Parsons accounts for far too much too easily by appealing to his notion of *structural differentiation*. He does not make use of the idea in the present address, but it is clear from reading his other works that structural differentiation is the basis for an important segment of the view presented in this address. "Differentiation refers to the process by which simple structures are divided into functionally differing components, these components becoming relatively independent of one another, and then recombined into more complex structures in which the functions of the differentiated units are complementary." (Talcott Parsons, "Youth in the Context of American Society," *Daedalus*, 1962, p. 103.) Using this

device, later developments in any institutional sphere can always turn out to be derivations from the previous situation, exactly "what one would expect." Parsons has stressed the phenomenon of structural differentiation primarily in connection with the economic order, the family, and the religious aspect of American culture. He has been criticized in regard to this, in that the result of differentiation is believed to be an atomized mass society; but Parsons himself indicates that the result of differentiation is "an increasingly ramified network of criss-crossing solidarities," which leads to a *pluralist* society, not an atomized mass society. Cf. his "The Link Between Character and Society," written with Winston White, in *Social Structure and Personality* (The Free Press of Glencoe, Inc., 1964), pp. 183–235.

10. Cf. William Kolb, "Images of Men and the Sociology of Religion," *Journal for the Scientific Study Of Religion*, Vol. I (1961–1962), pp. 5–22. This is followed by Talcott Parsons' response.

11. Bernard R. Berelson and G. A. Steiner, *Human Behavior: An Inventory of Scientific Findings* (Harcourt, Brace and World, Inc., 1964), p. 663.

12. *Ibid.*, p. 665.

13. *Ibid.*, p. 666.

14. *Ibid.*, p. 667.

15. *Ibid.*

16. *Ibid.*

17. Berelson and Steiner are not, of course, responsible for the use I have made of their conclusion. For all I know, they would repudiate what I have said.

V

THE PUBLIC RESPONSIBILITY

OF THEOLOGY

Roger L. Shinn

Let us start by distinguishing between the public responsibility of theology and the public splash made by theology. Not every splash is a responsibility. The theologian, who is as eager as the next man to nurse his ego, may enjoy the splash without accepting the responsibility. Sometimes, of course, a public responsibility involves a public splash, but not always. Responsibility and splash are neither identical nor mutually exclusive.

There have been times of great public splash in the history of theology—times of public attention for the theologian, times when theology came close to making good a claim to be "queen of the sciences." Those were not necessarily better days for theology.

Today theologians do not commonly complain that too many people are excited about theology. But this was exactly the complaint of Gregory of Nyssa in the days of the Arian controversy. He was bothered that all sorts and conditions of men had become "off-hand dogmatists in theology": "mere mechanics, . . . servants too and slaves that have been flogged, runaways from servile work," clothes vendors, moneylenders, food salesmen. Apparently nobody wanted to sell to Gregory the normal products and services of urbane life without giving him theological advice, perhaps as the equivalent of trading stamps. "Enquire the price of bread, he answers: Greater is the Father, and the Son is subject. Say that a bath would suit you, and he defines that the Son is made out of nothing!"[1]

Whether Gregory's complaint was snobbish or justified, it is not the complaint of most theologians today. Our salesmen and taxi drivers are not schooled in theological small talk or profundities.

The ancient complaints about excessive theological disputation came not only from theologians but also from pagans. One fourth-century historian, Marcellinus of Antioch, expressed his annoyance at the consequences of the fervid theological involvement of Constantius II:

> As his delight in complicated theological hair-splitting was greater than his sense of responsibility for maintaining harmony, he provoked innumerable dissensions, and he added fuel to the galloping flames by organizing acrimonious debates. One consequence was that crowds of prelates made use of the public post-horses for rushing to and fro on the business of these "synods," as they called them. The prelates' object was to wrench the whole practice of their religion into conformity with their own caprice; Constantius's achievement was to ham-string the postal service.[2]

Times have changed. Occasionally at the airport, following some sizable church meeting, I have seen standbys who, if they had known why that specific flight was crowded, might have agreed with Marcellinus that churchmen travel too much. And occasionally the Vatican Council or an Assembly of the World Council of Churches has prompted considerable public discussion of theological issues related to religious liberty, understanding of Judaism, the appraisal of Communism, the use of nuclear energy, the population explosion, social justice, etc. But we are far from the time of Nicaea with its widespread popular discussion and fanaticism on intricate dogmatic issues. And most of us are not sorry. Some past public roles of theology we do not recognize as our responsibilities today.

As a matter of fact, most theologians were more embarrassed

than pleased when, some years ago, *The New York Times Book Review* carried on its best-seller list for 186 weeks—the longest stretch "within the recent memory of man," the *Times* said— a book called *The Power of Positive Thinking.* They did not consider this to be a theological book, but they were afraid some of the public might. And theologians did not crave the fame or notoriety coming out of such a public judgment.

Why Theology Has a Public Responsibility

Theology necessarily has a public responsibility because the Christian gospel is public. The ministry of Jesus was a public event. His public included intimate friends and scheming enemies, religious officials and disreputable sinners, crowds of people who sometimes hailed him and sometimes jeered him, government officials and an army of occupation. Furthermore, faith has always understood this ministry to have a public aim. It was directed toward the world. "For God so loved the world that he gave his only Son." (John 3:16.)

Theology, then, has the purpose of thinking about this public event and—in at least some sense—of thinking for the sake of the public (the world). That responsibility is inherent in the nature of the gospel.

Furthermore, theology in fact emerges out of a dialogue between gospel and culture. Traditionally, theology has given great attention to the relation of faith and reason. Without discarding this formulation of the issue, I think a more contemporary statement of it may be in terms of gospel and culture. I speak of gospel because Christian faith, however much it gets mixed up in practice with everything else, is response to a gospel that is given. And I speak of culture because we now recognize that our reason is not some pure reason, abstractly ingrained in us; it is an acculturated reason, sometimes a set of cultural habits and attitudes somewhat rationalized. So theology comes out of the interaction of gospel and culture. It arises out of dialogue and it engages in dialogue.

In this dialogue, theology cannot be the answer book for the questions of a waiting public. I doubt that it ever was. Certainly it cannot be so today, both because the public is rarely waiting in expectation for theology to speak and because theology does not have the prefabricated answers for the questions the public is asking. Yet the participation in the public dialogue is important because theology has a contribution to make and because its integrity demands involvement. In public engagement theology may contribute to some clarification and purification of men's understanding and purposes; likewise, it may gain clarification and purification from the participation.

The public or significant interests within it may resent theological participation or intrusion, and the resentment needs careful examination. On one occasion in recent American history a group of clergymen volunteered to serve as mediators in a labor dispute. The corporation involved agreed to accept their services, subject to one condition: that labor and management then be invited to settle the arguments among the clergymen. A company spokesman reports with some glee, "We never heard another word from them."

That episode recalls an earlier event in England, reported by William Temple:

> When a group of Bishops attempted to bring Government, Coal-Owners and Miners together in a solution of the disastrous Coal Strike of 1926, Mr. Baldwin, then Prime Minister, asked how the Bishops would like it if he referred to the Iron and Steel Federation the revision of the Athanasian Creed, and this was acclaimed as a legitimate score.[3]

In such polemics at least two issues need to be distinguished. The first is that of the public interest. A private argument, whether about wages and hours, about doctrine, or about anything else, can be left to the parties concerned—up to a point. But if the dispute begins to harm people and disturb the public interest, then the public has a stake in it. At that point the participants cannot tell everyone else to mind his own business. The second issue concerns competence to make judgments. There are eco-

nomic issues on which theologians, as theologians, have no competence—and doctrinal issues on which corporation executives, as
corporation executives, lack competence. Then anybody who
enters into the discussion had better make himself competent.
But in precisely this area of distinctions of function and
competence, we run into difficulty. The distinctions that can
abstractly be drawn so neatly are far less clear in the areas of
public policy. The theological and ethical issues in the common
life are inseparable from the entire fabric of that common life.
When Elijah attacked King Ahab and Queen Jezebel, the least
cogent answer of the monarchs would have been to say: "Run
along, prophet, and stick to your business of religion. We'll
stick to running the state. Then neither of us need get in the
other's way."

The distinguished economist, John Maynard Keynes, once wrote
to Archbishop Temple that the Archbishop, in arguing that the
church should be concerned about political and economic issues,
had actually *understated* his case. "There are practically no issues
of policy as distinct from technique which do not involve ethical
considerations. If this is emphasized, the right of the Church to
interfere in what is essentially a branch of ethics becomes even
more obvious."⁴

The issue of competence is often confused. We are all too
familiar with cases where clerical judgments turn into foolish or
abstract moralizing because the judges deliver verdicts without
understanding the intricate facts of a social situation. Thus churchmen may moralize about the national debt without understanding the function of credit in our society or the relation of government debt to fiscal policy and the functioning of the economy.
They may in times of social conflict advocate an illusory peace
that perpetuates injustice, because they do not understand the
real dynamics of the social process. They may condemn the mis-
behavior of specific groups—e.g., protestors against racial discrimination, infractions of civil rights, or the draft—without examining the reasons for the protests. It is entirely too tempting

to make moral judgments without doing the hard work necessary if those judgments are to be cogent.

On the other hand, it is equally easy to abdicate moral responsibility by turning the judgments over to experts. Two of the world's most prominent social scientists have recently made this point emphatically, specifically with reference to international policy. Gunnar Myrdal, in an article entitled "With What Little Wisdom the World Is Ruled,"[5] argues that the follies of foreign policy are heightened by the public disposition to trust the judgments of the insiders who make the decisions:

> One reason why the ordinary citizen is often prepared to abdicate his own judgment over foreign policy is that he tends to assume that the government has information of a secret nature, not available to the general public. . . . Experience suggest that outside of purely military matters the belief is vastly exaggerated when it is not entirely false.

Similarly, Hans Morgenthau has warned against "the intellectual defeatism and political apathy" that follow from the assumption that only a scientific elite know enough about public policy to make intelligent decisions. Hence, he urges that we not leave the major decisions to the experts:

> The expert does *not* know more about the likely political and military effects of the great technological decisions of our age than the man in the street or the politically responsible official would know were they endowed with technologically informed common sense. . . . The politically aware scientist, then, has no advantage over the scientifically informed layman; and if the former is not politically aware he is even inferior to the latter.[6]

Obviously I am not arguing that theologians should determine public policy. I am saying that they have a responsibility to enter into the processes of public discussion that determine policy. This is a society that in its pledge of allegiance to the flag declares that it lives "under God." Although the theologian has no unique insight into the meaning of life under God, his professional task is to study the meaning of belief in God and life under God. He is negligent in his responsibility if he does not engage in public discussion at those points where the common life has theological and ethical significance. In doing so, he will find that there are not many points where this life does not have such significance.

Christian faith has characteristically refused to separate private from public life. Of course, it can make valid and important distinctions. The Christian knows better than to suppose that he can transform his personal responsibility of worship and prayer into a public obligation upon the society. Society rightly resists some intrusions of religion into the public domain, and religion rightly resists some intrusions of society into the realm of personal freedom. Because of imperialistic, even totalitarian, impulses in both religion and society, it has taken the Christian community and the civil community many centuries of agonizing history to learn this lesson. We need to keep learning it. But we mislearn it when we assume that the legitimate privacy of faith means that faith has no public meaning.

This issue came in for considerable discussion during the presidential campaign of 1960. John F. Kennedy found it necessary to dissociate himself from that strand in Roman Catholic teaching—certainly not the only strand—which had long opposed religious liberty and had sought for a church-dominated state. He did so—most of us believe truthfully and effectively. In seeking to get rid of a double burden—of a tradition within his church and of prejudice from outside his church—he sometimes overstated his case, to the extent of insisting that religion was irrelevant to the exercise of public office. In his famous meeting with the Houston clergy, he said, in the midst of many fine things: "I believe in a President whose views on religion are his own private affair." In the heat of a campaign it would probably have been futile to insist on more subtle distinctions. But the religious views of a candidate become a legitimate subject of public concern *at any points* where those views impinge upon public policy. In a campaign it is certainly better to debate the opinions on policy than the theology and faith that lie behind them. But it is a curious recommendation of a candidate to argue that his faith could not possibly influence his political judgment. That recommendation was made at more than one point in the campaign of 1960. One prominent clergyman publicly opposed Kennedy because of the Roman Catholic doctrine of church and state. Later, it is only fair to say, he publicly renounced this judgment. But on the occasion of his initial statement, he was asked by the press whether Richard Nixon's Quaker faith might disqualify him as Commander in Chief of the Army. The clergyman thought not. "I don't think he ever let it bother him," he said. That offhand comment, intended to be favorable to the candidate, was probably not meant to convey so much as it said. But if anyone were to take it seriously, it would be a devastating judgment.

I am saying that it is important but not easy to distinguish the public from the private meanings of faith. Although I say this as a theological conviction, I am sure that the difficulty is not created by theology. Social psychology and cultural anthropology in our time are showing us the rich and intricate relationship between the person and his society. Like theology, they are saying that there is a difference between the two, but most of our habitual statements of the difference are far too simple to be accurate. In this insight they are consistent—although usually not intentionally so—with Biblical faith. As a single example, we might consider the Magnificat. This hymn of the early church, presented by Luke as the "Song of Mary" when she learns that she is to be the mother of Jesus, unites the private and the public in a characteristically Biblical way. As the poem of rejoicing of one Jewish girl expecting to become a mother, the Magnificat is intensely personal. Its language begins with phrases in the first person singular: "My soul . . . my spirit . . . my Savior . . . for me." But soon the Magnificat is talking about the history of the nations: about a God who "has put down the mighty from their thrones, and exalted those of low degree." In the Magnificat, as in Scripture generally, there is nothing bizarre about this association of the personal and the public. God is Lord of his whole creation.

Some Consequences

I have been maintaining that theology has a responsibility to participate in the discussion of all public issues, seeking to illumine their theological and ethical meanings. I am not maintaining that the theologian should abandon his professional task to become an amateur political or military strategist. Whatever competence he can gain in fields outside his own may enhance his ability to see the theological dimensions of those fields. But his professional competence remains primarily in theology.

Let us, therefore, look at some specific tasks that he may undertake in exercising his public responsibility.

1. The Teaching of Theology

I have already said that "theology has the purpose—in at least some sense—of thinking for the sake of the public." Its work is not simply thinking about a strictly defined subject matter—say, the Bible or traditional doctrines. It thinks about human existence as illuminated and changed by the Biblical message. Human existence is everybody's business. Theology aims to identify and clarify certain issues of human existence. It does so in the faith that God addresses man in all his existence and has addressed him in a quite specific way in the Biblical revelation. Thus it enters into the conversation between gospel and culture (as mentioned earlier in this paper), seeking to formulate with some adequacy the Christian faith.

This formulation is in large part a teaching function. It is a function both for the faithful and for the society at large. The community of faith has a special stake in the understanding and clarifying of its faith, and the theologian may address himself to this community—the traditional function of dogmatics. But the community also has a concern that outsiders understand it with some adequacy, so that they can decide responsibly whether they want to share this faith or not—the traditional function of apologetics.[7] In the last analysis I do not think dogmatics and apologetics can be separated. Dogmatics, even in the strictest sense of the term, must address the skeptic within the community of faith and the skeptic within the dogmatic theologian.

Notice that I have not said that the theologian first formulates doctrine, then if he is so inclined, teaches it. I have said instead that the formulation is in large part a teaching function. Doctrine cannot be formulated apart from conversation. There is no Word of God that is not a Word of communication. The Word that once took flesh in a man of words and deeds must by its nature continually seek enfleshment in the thought and life of man.

Hence, theology must ceaselessly break out of its own ghettoes. Paul Tillich loved an idea of Nietzsche's—that "no idea could be true unless it was thought in the open air."[8] There is a striking similarity between that metaphor and Pope John XXIII's throwing open of the Vatican windows as a symbol of his hopes for the Vatican Council.

All this means that I think there is something wrongheaded in the desire of many theologians to think and write for their theological colleagues rather than for the public. Let me quickly grant the validity of part of their case. An intellectually rigorous theology (the only kind of theology worth anything) must develop a vocabulary and set of methods comparable to those of every other intellectual discipline. Specialists will learn the vocabulary and methods; they will want their work scrutinized and criticized by other specialists. So they will work—as physicists, art critics, and sociologists work—with a vocabulary incomprehensible to most of the public. But if that is the only way they work, they will be neglecting the basis of theology, the conversation between gospel and culture.

Hence, I would say that the rejection of the effort to write theology for the public is a pusillanimous action. To my learned colleagues who disdain "popularizing," I reply that some popularizing is cheap and some is good, just as some technical writing is cheap and some is good. It may help to distinguish two methods of writing theology for the public. I would reject any method that neglects intellectual rigor for the sake of easier success. But assuming the importance of the intellectual task, I suggest a distinction. There is the process of thinking through a subject in a technical way, then deciding how much of it can be translated into a more popular version. This is a type of writing that is done in medicine and in science, and it can be done in theology. It is a legitimate way—the way, for example, of Calvin's *Instruction in Faith* as contrasted with his *Institutes*.

The other method I think is more important. This requires the theologian to think through an issue with the greatest technical competence he can command. Then—or even better, simultaneously —he thinks it through in another way—the way of the poet, of the parent, of the man making a decision. And with due regard for all these ways he tries to write his thoughts for the public.

What impresses me is that most of the great theologians wrote for the public in one or the other of these ways. Think of Augustine, Luther, Calvin, Barth, Tillich, Niebuhr. The lesser thinkers have often refused to do so, lest they lose the prestige of scholars. Theological scholarship, if it would stay honest, needs the discipline both of writing for the theological fraternity and of writing for the public.

2. The Interdisciplinary and Intercultural Conversation

In addressing the public, theology has a peculiar responsibility in a time of intellectual and cultural fragmentation. In past ages theology aspired to the ideal of building an architectonic synthesis of human understanding. No theologian—perhaps nobody at all—aspires to that role anymore. It has become common to say that theology should now seek to be not queen of the sciences but servant of them all. I am willing to accept that change of assignment, provided the servant may be a little less deferential, a little more annoying than servants are normally expected to be. Theology by its nature must maintain a lively interest in many human interests. Therefore, it has a stake in interdisciplinary conversations. It is not permitted to exploit the other disciplines for its own purposes, as though they had no inner logic and no independent value of their own. But it must keep alert to what they are doing. It will appropriate some of their findings, and it will ask persistent questions about the meaning and worth of many human activities.

In the university world these days we are all familiar with, and perhaps a little worried by, C. P. Snow's thesis of the two cultures. There have been many criticisms and elaborations of the basic idea, but I think nobody has denied that Snow was getting at a real problem. I suggest that theology has a strategic place in this problem. Working in a university setting, I find that my students and I must keep making forays into the major divisions of the university: the humanities, the social sciences, and the natural sciences. Religion, as an academic discipline, is usually placed among the humanities, because in its dealing with human aspirations it has obvious kinship with literature and the fine arts. Certainly it must inquire into and ask the meaning of the accounts of human existence given by tragedians, novelists, lyric poets, and painters. Yet its connection with the social sciences is equally important. No theologian would try to develop a doctrine of man without considering what psychologists have said. He cannot deal with social ethics in ignorance of the work of economists, sociologists, and political theorists. Finally, if he has any serious concern for truth, he cannot pretend that the theological conception of God and the universe has no connection with the natural sciences. He must take account of the current comeback in metaphysics and note the scientific interest involved. Thus theology seeks to foster conversations between the two—or three or many—cultures that fragment the world of the modern intellect.

In another sense theology must enter into intercultural conversations. Most of the actual work of theology is done in the world of the affluent intellectual. Individual theologians, of course, can moan about their poverty as well as anybody else. They rarely are looking for places to put idle risk capital. But most of them have tenure, pleasant homes, and comfortable working conditions. Few of them belong to the impoverished fourth or fifth of our affluent society, and few belong to the impoverished majority of our world.

But because of the Christian gospel, they are constrained to be concerned about the poor, the frustrated, the victims of discrimination in a cruel world. They have a task, rarely well executed, of keeping alive conversation between the cultures of deprivation and the cultures of the affluent intellectuals. It is at this point that the civil rights movement has made its great contribution to save theology from stultification. Whatever theology has done for the civil rights movement is less than the movement has done for theology.

3. The Public Political Conversation

In describing the theological contribution to the public political conversation, let me return to the thesis that I stated early in this paper. "The theological and ethical issues in the common life are inseparable from the entire fabric of that common life." Quoting John Maynard Keynes, I argued that theology has every right to participate in the public debate on political and economic issues. I insisted that theological spokesmen acquire some competence in the concrete issues of the common life that they discuss. Now I want to distinguish that part of the public conversation in which the theologian has specific competence. Any theologian may acquire competence in economics, geopolitics, or political theory, but these skills are not part of his theological skill as such. The crucial point in public debate where the theologian should have competence, as theologian, is the criticism of ideology. And this ideological area is fundamental to most public debate.

The theologian may or may not have skill in proposing public policy on such issues as the elimination of poverty, medical care for the aged, rehabilitation of housing, or the national policy in Southeast Asia. He has the right of any citizen to discuss these issues, and if he has studied them with care, his judgments may be weighty. As Myrdal and Morgenthau have suggested, the educated citizen should not be reluctant to take up issues like these.

But I am suggesting that the specific professional qualifications of the theologian equip him most directly to be the critic of the ideologies that operate in all such debates. He is in particular the critic of the Christian heresies that dominate so much of American thinking.

With some trepidation I suggest that theology today is called to an effective job of heresy-hunting. I am not talking about persecution of heretics, but simply about the identification of heresy. Since there has recently been talk in the American church of heresy trials, let me say that I do not advocate the censure of thinkers who unabashedly examine Christian teachings to see where they need revision in our time—a practice that the church has always carried out and needs to carry out today. I mean the distortion of Christian faith to serve political and ideological ends that actually oppose the deepest meaning of this faith.

I mean, for example, the nationalism that infects so much of American policy—not simply the recognition of a national interest that is always involved in foreign policy, but the implicit assumption that our nation is the proper adjudicator of the national interest of peoples everywhere in the world. Theology may not be competent to prescribe a Latin American policy; many nontheological skills are needed for the prescription. But theology has a public responsibility to unveil ideologies that influence Latin American policy. Thus in September the United States House of Representatives, after all of forty minutes of debate, passed a resolution stating that any country in the hemisphere may use armed force in any other country to answer the threat of Communism. Everybody knew that the resolution had no legal force and that it was worded so vaguely as to justify practically any kind of intervention. It was a pure act of piety, and as piety it was either sheer paganism or malignant heresy.

Again, I mean the kind of heresy that reduces God to a kindly accomplice to our purposes. The heresy is so widespread that when I take a vivid example, I am not implying unique guilt to anybody. Recently one state—it happened to be Kansas—ran a nationwide advertising campaign to attract industry. Its message was that "Kansas developed the 'Great Society' long ago!" The explanation said: "In Kansas the 'Great Society' means Great People, people who want to work for a living, people who give a day's work for a day's pay, people who believe in God, people who believe in each other, people who believe in free enterprise, people who believe in America." Any scholar might puzzle over the empirical verification. Do more Kansans than Georgians believe in God? The theologian must also wonder about the use of God—a use that must be more offensive to the God and Father of our Lord Jesus Christ than quantities of talk that candidly rejects him.

Still again, I mean the idolatry of law and order as the ultimate criteria of moral action. From the time when the Supreme Court made its historic decision on public school segregation in 1954, many churchmen who knew that segregation was theologically wrong quit saying so. It was easier to appeal to law and order than to the faith of the church. In a pluralistic society there are times when it is more appropriate to ask society to heed the Supreme Court than to call upon Christian authority. But at least in the church the authority of law cannot be confused with the authority of God. Yet just this happened, so that many churchmen had no preparation to evaluate acts of civil disobedience. Journalists like David Lawrence and Raymond Moley express bewilderment that clergymen should be participating in civil disobedience, a bewilderment that an hour with the Bible ought to clear up. The decision about the occasion that calls for civil disobedience requires the utmost of conscientious thought. But the theological judgment that should be utterly clear is that the Christian, although he may not take a cavalier attitude toward

THE PUBLIC RESPONSIBILITY OF THEOLOGY

civil government, can never let the laws of society become the final definition of obedience to God.

At this particular time in American history theology has a responsibility to impress upon the society the importance of dissent. Theology does not, I have suggested above, have responsibility for devising a policy for Vietnam. It is not responsible to agree with everyone who demonstrates against our policy or burns a draft card. It does have responsibility for interpreting to the public the meaning of dissent and the value of conscience. Theology needs to help the public understand the individual who, against all social pressures, finds himself impelled to oppose the actions of his government.

As a final example, I mean the curious version of individualism that has so often gained ideological power in our society. Although it has nothing to do with the Christian concern for the person who gets lost in the competition or the system, it is often confused with Christian personalism or Protestant individualism. Thus in the presidential campaign of 1964 many of the supporters of Barry Goldwater, assuming that his brand of individualism was authentic Protestant Christianity, were utterly and honestly amazed at the opposition to him from prominent churchmen. The surprise was possible only because theology had not accomplished its public responsibility.

Recently our Roman Catholic friends, who have often done better on this particular issue, have run into the same problem. In 1965, William Buckley, who had once written a book about God at Yale, ran for mayor of New York on the Conservative ticket, taking up roughly the same cause that Mr. Goldwater had sought to enhance. At one point in the campaign the Catholic Timothy Costello, running for office on the Lindsay fusion ticket, said that Mr. Buckley was actually opposed to the Catholic social teachings. This statement was generally regarded as a campaign gaffe. But as one Jesuit political scientist told me, Mr. Costello was undoubtedly accurate, even though he was probably not wise to say what he did. My point is that, if a candidate should not state this truth during a campaign, maybe a theologian should. Or if it is unwise for the theologian to intrude upon the campaign argument, theologians should be constantly helping the church and the public to recognize heretical doctrines when politicians advocate them.

The public responsibility of theology is a responsibility loaded with hazards. It is no task for the unwary. But, then, theology is no undertaking for the unwary. It is always possible for theology to make erroneous judgments in the public arena, but it is just as possible to make errors on technical points of doctrine. Since God is Lord of all life—not simply of some segment boxed off and labeled religion—theology has a public responsibility. In the exercise of that responsibility, it should establish rigorous standards of competence; then it should do its job. There is always the risk of error and even infidelity in exercising this public responsibility. But there is the certainty of error and infidelity in the alternative of irresponsibility.

NOTES

1. B. J. Kidd, ed., *Documents Illustrative of the History of the Church* (London: SCM Press, Ltd., 1920), Vol. II, p. 135.

2. Ammianus Marcellinus, *Res Gestae*, XXI. xvi. 18, as quoted by Arnold J. Toynbee, *A Study of History*, 12 vols. (Oxford University Press, 1935–1961), Vol. VII, p. 96.

3. William Temple, *Christianity and Social Order* (Penguin Books, Inc., 1942), p. 7.

4. John Maynard Keynes, letter of December 3, 1941, in F. A. Iremonger, *William Temple, Archbishop of Canterbury: His Life and Letters* (London: Oxford University Press, 1948), pp. 438–449.

5. *The New York Times Magazine*, July 18, 1965.

6. Hans Morgenthau, "The Consequences of Science," *Current*, April, 1965, pp. 28–29; reprinted from "Modern Science and Political Power," *Columbia Law Review*, December, 1964, pp. 1407–1409.

7. Much of the traditional apologetics gave more emphasis to persuasion or argument than I am giving. I do not oppose

these activities; in a world where everybody is persuading and arguing, I think theology has a perfect right to do so too. But I put more emphasis upon clarifying than upon persuading. If men are accepting or rejecting Christian faith, they should have some idea of what they are accepting or rejecting.

8. Paul Tillich, *The Interpretation of History* (Charles Scribner's Sons, 1936), p. 8.

V A

THEOLOGY IN DIALOGUE

Bernardin J. Patterson

Throughout our land clergymen of all faiths have proved their belief in the living word of God by actively taking part in social movements designed to further the common good. The civil rights movement, for example, attests to their balanced involvement not only as Americans, but also as theologians. They believe that the churches and the theological profession have a public responsibility and that this role involves the articulating and the stirring of the moral conscience of mankind.

Dr. Roger Shinn has done a masterful job of defining the nature and principles of the exercise of this theological responsibility. Indicative of his sensitivity and perception is the emphasis on the teaching role of theology, when he takes up the specific tasks of this discipline. Balanced teaching involves three distinct but related functions: *research,* in which the boundaries of truth are pushed forward; *instruction,* in which a discipline is taught to professional students with as much technical accuracy as is possible; and *service of the public,* or "the care of souls." Dr. Shinn has shown that theological research implies the formulation of teaching through dialogue, and it is this insight that weds the teaching task to the task of interdisciplinary and intercultural conversation. It would be a poor practical theologian who neglected discoveries in the fields of psychology and mass media communication. Similarly, the specialist in Christian ethics or moral theology must be conversant with the assured results of sociology. Dr. Shinn makes this point well. There is, however, a more urgent consideration to which he simply alludes: the dethronement of theology has led imperceptibly to a very real abasement.

Dr. Charles C. Josey, Professor Emeritus of Psychology at Butler University, in addressing the Indianapolis chapter of the Academy of Religion and Science on the subject of "The Role of Religion in Healing," pointed out the fact that the Journal of the Academy had carried a broad range of articles over the years on psychology and psychiatric techniques, but few, if any, articles on the role of religion in healing. Conversation with psychiatrists inevitably turned into monologue, with the psychiatrist lecturing and answering humble questions. The common presupposition in these attempts at dialogue has been that the psychiatrist or psychologist had numerous valuable insights, but that the theologian could offer little of worth to the discussion.

We do indeed advocate interdisciplinary and intercultural conversation, but we feel that it should no longer remain a one-way street. Theologians themselves must be the first to discover their resources and the possibilities of valid contribution to interdisciplinary exchanges. It will be difficult for the natural scientists, social scientists, and even mythmakers of our day to take us seriously as twentieth-century men if we theologians fail to envision ourselves in such a role. Dialogue implies dual identity. Our problem is not so much in discovering the identity of the social scientists and naturalists or humanists, but in discovering our own authentic being. We have yet to begin to believe that we have something valid to give. In the final section of his paper Dr. Shinn discusses one important contribution that theology can make, namely, the criticizing of the ideologies that operate in public debate. This is a point well taken, since without our aid few men would be able to question the underlying assumptions —the accepted frames of reference—of public discussion. Most public discussion is conducted by means of the mass media; thus the effective prophets of our age are the journalists and news commentators. We are, therefore, faced with the dilemma that though we have a role that we should play, others have pre-empted it because of their strategic position in our society. Reflections such as these may seem to be negative in the extreme. They do, however, demand that we take a realistic look into today's needs and trends. Only in this way can we pursue the dialogue between the gospel and culture—our mid-twentieth-century culture.

There are mixed feelings whenever we dwell upon the fact, but it is a fact, that our society is guided by the Federal Government. This deep federal involvement in social welfare, hospitalization, education, communications, industry, and civil rights was necessitated by several factors. America is essentially pluralistic. The refusal of the Protestant Establishment to recognize this fact—witness the founding of a Federal, then a "National," Council of Churches, which fails to include the largest single church group in North America—and the ghetto mentality of American Catholics made it impossible for Protestants, Catholics, and Jews to organize for joint action in areas that were claimed as the special province of religion: hospitalization, moral education, youth guidance, population control, human rights, and the like. The divisions, suspicions, and hostilities of the various faith groups rendered them ineffective in carrying out the corporal and spiritual works of mercy; hence, government has had to take the lead in conceiving programs and in bringing the social-action leaders of the three faiths together for mutual cooperation. In 1959, when Mr. Eisenhower was contemplating the passage of the second civil rights law since the Reconstruction, he asked Vice-President Nixon to call together the heads of the national religious social agencies. On November 17, 1959, representatives of the National Conference of Catholic Charities, the Council of Jewish Federations and Welfare Funds, and the Social Welfare Department of the National Council of Churches met under the auspices of the Federal Government to discuss the ways in which organized religion might assist in procuring the rights of all Americans as free men and citizens. The result was a law authorizing the establishment of local and state commissions on human rights to cooperate with the United States Commission on Civil Rights. During the past six years these White House conferences have continued to be called twice each year to gain the support of religious agencies for federal programs in the areas of poverty, civil rights, medical care, and education. Any realistic approach to seminary education today must plan curriculum and extracurricular activities to train seminarians for interfaith cooperation in all efforts of community concern, but even more importantly the theological students must be made aware of the social legislation and programs of the federal, state, and local governments, and they must be given experience in some of the 190 federal programs now operating in the social and educational fields. There are sixteen federal programs in the area of housing alone, and more and more the churches and synagogues will find themselves exercising an ancillary role to stabilize communities and to provide or restore homes. This is but one indication that courses in moral theology and social action and ethics need to concern themselves much more about federal programs and laws than about episcopal and papal pronouncements. The President and the Supreme Court have become in effect the representatives of the conscience of the entire pluralistic American nation, and, whether we like the idea or not, we can do little that is constructive unless we see our role in the social field as preparatory to and consequent upon federal authority.

The religious pluralism of our country as well as the development of industrial technology necessitated large-scale federal involvement in the social and educational fields, but this pluralism has had another result. It has placed the layman (the banker, lawyer, realtor, investor) in the position of top community leadership and reduced the clergyman to a counselor, organizer, and teacher. It is the layman who exercises effective power in determining in what direction a community will go; hence, the layman has emancipated himself from clerical authority in all the really important decisions of life. Theological education must recognize this emancipation of the laity and aim at aiding the layman to use his freedom well and wisely. Religious pluralism has also emancipated theology. New contacts with other great religions have taught Christians and Jews how much they share in common with the rest of mankind. These contacts have also given new perspective, historical and anthropological, to our view of religious teaching. We see that freedom in theology is as important as freedom in science, with only truth as the authority, norm, and limiting factor. There may be " 'one Lord, one faith, one baptism' [Eph. 4:5], but a variety of theologies," remarks Pater Hans Küng in his noted lecture on "Freedom in Theology." The regimentation and narrowness of the controversial post-Reformation theology must be replaced by a broad, inquiring, open approach to the science of divine things.

Although I cannot enlarge upon these points here, I would like to mention that a new type of theological orientation is required by the fact that our society is multiracial, science-directed, sports-oriented, and entertainment conscious.

VB

TOWARD A THEOLOGY
OF PUBLIC RESPONSIBILITY

Creighton Lacy

Many of you, I suspect, share with me a profound empathy for the most widely read theological faculty in America today—Peanuts. Some time ago Charlie Brown reassured Lucy about a seemingly endless deluge of rain by citing the promise of God to Noah, recalled in the rainbow. Lucy with her devastating sarcasm replied: "You've taken a great load off my mind." For once Charlie Brown had a comeback. "Sound theology," he explained very seriously, "has a way of doing that."

One need not join the "peace of mind" cult to accept that observation. If at times we have had great loads laid upon our minds instead of taken off, that, too, is at least part of "the public responsibility of theology." For a long time after I first heard about this symposium, I had difficulty remembering whether it was to deal with "America and the Future of Theology" or "Theology and the Future of America"—perhaps because the two are so frequently confused in our contemporary society.

Fortunately, among all the spokesmen for sound theology in this tangled world of ours, none speaks with greater clarity, profound simplicity, and compelling directness than Roger Shinn. No one who knows him or this characteristic about him would undertake the role of commentator without making very sure that the assignment called for "development in whatever direction seems to you most appropriate" rather than for presumptive or pre-

sumptuous disagreement. Dr. Shinn is undeniably one of those
rare theologians about whom he himself speaks, one who can
"think through an issue with the greatest competence" yet simultaneously as a poet, a parent, a politician; one who displays the
art of both thinking and "writing for the theological fraternity
and the public." His statements are always so judicious and his
views so thoroughly akin to mine that there is no place to stand
except on common ground.

My own remarks, therefore, will be of two kinds: some areas
of hearty and grateful endorsement with an occasional additional
illustration; and second, but interspersed, a few derivative questions
that seem to me crucial enough to deserve further enlightenment.
There has been—and I believe can be—no quarrel with the primary thesis that "theology necessarily has a public responsibility."
But I am not fully satisfied with Dr. Shinn's explication of why
this is so—or how this is so. The public nature of the incarnation,
of Christ's ministry, of the world arena, is clear and incontro-
vertible. And he defines the gospel as a "given" that is somehow
set over against, or at least in dialogue with, culture. But between
the declaration that "responsibility is inherent in the nature of the
gospel" and the assertion that "its integrity demands involvement"
lie somewhat pragmatic, utilitarian, factual assumptions which
need to be elucidated further. Especially in the context of these
proceedings, where theology has been approached and defined—if
at all—from a variety of standpoints, one may legitimately inquire what *kind* of theology demands involvement or possesses
inherent responsibility.

A closely related question, which emerges from the opening
sentences of Dr. Shinn's paper and against the background of his
predecessors, concerns the relation of "the new theology" to "the
new morality." Admittedly neither is strictly new. As Dr. Altizer
goes back quite frankly to Blake and Hegel and Nietzsche, so the
assumed freedom of contextual or situational ethics has affinities
with Schleiermacher, Marx, and other nineteenth-century thinkers—not to mention the New Testament. But within our contemporary maelstrom I am still trying to discover whether the new

morality—so-called—is an inevitable consequence of an allegedly godless theology (at least the abandonment of transcendent norms), or whether, conversely, the new theology is an effort to provide a "religious" sanction for an ethic that rejects all deontological reference, in natural law or legalistic codes.

We are told that theological participation must recognize both public interest and private competence. Wholeheartedly agreed! But I am surprised and a trifle bothered by the strictly negative definition of public interest: "if the dispute begins to harm people and disturb." True, Dr. Shinn had previously pointed out the necessity for public responsibility, and he went on to list specific areas of obligation. But if the realm of theology is as broad as he implies, then surely there are more positive imperatives to justify its "intrusion" into allegedly private and "nontheological" matters.

On the issue of competence, Roger Shinn's strictures should eliminate a great deal of misunderstanding—or misrepresentation. We are all aware of how often churchmen are accused of speaking from ignorance. The World Order Study Conference in St. Louis (October 20–23, 1965) is a good case in point. Delegates from most of the major communions and ecumenical agencies presumed to make recommendations on such controversial questions as Vietnam, South Africa, world trade, arms control. Vociferous critics fail to realize that some of the churchmen had recently returned from a visit to Vietnam, that scores had spent years in the Far East, that still others had backgrounds of loyal and effective Government service. Their factual information might not be identical with that available to the State Department or the Pentagon, but many of them were no less experts, in the sense which Gunnar Myrdal and Hans Morgenthau had in mind (in Dr. Shinn's quotations above).

Nevertheless, granting that theologians do not and should not *determine* public policy, there are times when they *should* speak concretely and not content themselves with pious generalities. Take the above-mentioned Study Conference recommendations on India and Pakistan as an example. Two specific proposals for the Kashmir dilemma had been submitted (at the initiative, incidentally, of some distinguished Indians as well as Western authorities), one for autonomy under United Nations auspices, the other for permanent partition with the central valley, a tourists' paradise, internationalized.[1] If rumors are correct, certain conference officials and drafters of reports argued in private that no single "solution" should be endorsed which had not been worked out in committee, but then argued in public that the conference should not propose alternatives lest this appear uncertain or irresponsible. What was left was a vague promise to support "any initiatives being taken by . . . any . . . UN body" and "to explore the possibility of creative alternatives to the present deadlock."[2] For years our self-styled pundits have been telling their real Pandits that neutralism was immoral because it led in effect to neutrality between right and wrong. It *may* be that in Kashmir—and in Vietnam—we face the excruciating dilemma of appearing to yield to military force in order to achieve what we believe in our inmost hearts is the most humane and ethical of viable solutions. It is not enough to cry, "Peace! Peace!" when there is no constructive basis for peace.

Foreign policy is not the only sphere where the theologian—or the conscientious Christian layman—needs to place informed moral judgment in the same computer with scientific and technological data. It has taken *Life* magazine to convince some of us that vital medical decisions now being made—and many, many more in the years ahead—require ethical and theological guidelines. Dr. Kildare may currently wrestle with the choice of recipients for kidney transplants, for example, but he has not yet tackled the serious risk to donors or the psychological problems of receivers. The possibility of freezing bodies has actually arrived, but theology is hardly ready for its role in the crucial decisions involved. Many Christians have "made up their minds" about abortion, birth control, and the like, but artificial insemination, test-tube babies, alteration of genes, put man on the threshold of vast new moral decisions in medicine. Here again, as Dr. Shinn so wisely says, theology must do some tough homework if its judgments are to be cogent, but it must not abdicate its responsibility to scientific experts.

As Roger Shinn makes superbly clear with his two campaign credos, "it is important but not easy to distinguish the public from the private meanings of faith"—and applications of faith. The *Playboy* Philosophy, and others, have been crusading for more uniform and more realistic sex laws, for example. The church, by and large, has not faced the issue of the Wolfenden Report, whether sin and crime cannot and must not be sharply differentiated, whether law has the right to punish any private behavior by consenting adults. Christians may soon have to decide whether or not they agree with the Supreme Court decision that individual privacy "must be subordinated to the public interest in law enforcement" (as in the conviction based on peep holes in the ceiling of a men's room in Yosemite National Park).

To take another example, most churchmen of the liberal persuasion now agree with Dr. Shinn that the "personal responsibility of worship and prayer" cannot be transformed "into a public obligation upon society." But a few of us are still profoundly vexed about the implications of such a position. I refer here not to the threat of undermining religion—although I confess to grave doubts as to where lines can logically and legally be drawn in regard to chaplains, prayers in the Senate, etc. But I am not wholly convinced, as a democrat or as a Christian, that an individual's rights must be protected at the expense of the rights of the majority. In this vast, overlapping area of public and private life, I find myself arguing—with unaccountable conservatism—that selfish individuals as well as impersonal society may trespass on "the realm of personal freedom."

Turning to specific consequences, one can applaud the teaching function of theology and still appeal for a clearer recognition of the learning function. If dogmatics and apologetics cannot be separated, there is a sense in which both may inhibit the principal factor in Dr. Shinn's equation, namely, dialogue. If the teaching function is "both for the faithful and for the society at large," we need guidance, on one hand, as to how to persuade the world to listen. I look on his paper as a masterful introduction to the subject: "How theology can make itself worth listening to—or at least worthy of being listened to."

On the other hand, we are—in one sense—just beginning to enter the era of genuine dialogue, however old the word may be. For centuries theology has been so preoccupied with dogmatics and apologetics, with protecting orthodoxy, that it has not really dared to listen to the world. In the so-called younger churches, with which I am more familiar, the fear of syncretism, of absorption, of being simply overwhelmed by the surrounding hostile culture, has been so great that Christians have developed a ghetto mentality—a physical, intellectual, and spiritual isolation which has often proved stultifying, and which has laid the church open to charges of foreignism, irrelevance, otherworldliness—in short, of public *ir*responsibility.

Dr. Shinn applies this to America in terms of interdisciplinary and intercultural conversation. The stated aim of this conference includes dialogue with nontheological disciplines, and it is obvious that we are agreed on the necessity for this. But how we are to break down the dividing walls of hostility in the compartmentalized lives of most church people is a task demanding continual effort.

I am particularly intrigued by Roger Shinn's application of "intercultural" conversation to social and economic classes, for we have been very, very reluctant to admit that such barriers exist, not only within the church but within theology. Our concern "about the poor, the frustrated, the victims of discrimination" has indeed been expressed through sympathy and charity, more recently by actual participation in the civil rights movement. Entranced by the thought of what the movement has done for theology, I cannot help feeling that the net effect so far has been a paternalistic, self-righteous salving of conscience, and that we have a long way to go before there is any significant theological dialogue or interaction between races or classes in American society.

Another point in Dr. Shinn's paper which deserves emphasis

is the thesis that a theologian's crucial relevance and competence in public debate lies at the point of criticizing prevailing ideology. Harvey Cox was asked about this role in Eastern Europe, and he suggested that the very existence of the church in a communist society is a challenge and a rebuff to the entire Marxist 'ideology, whether there is freedom to verbalize this opposition or not.[3] How much greater obligation rests on us as Christians—as theologians, if you will—where the opportunity to criticize dominant ideologies is limited only by our faithfulness.

Under this heading, I am convinced that much of the misunderstanding and the condemnation of theological "intrusion" in public affairs stems from our failure to make clear that we *are* judging ideological assumptions rather than simply technical policies. Our pronouncements on Red China or sex laws or civil rights legislation are promptly and roundly condemned by many people—within our churches as well as outside—because they *seem* to advocate specific policy *rather* than Christian principle. Or I should say "without Christian principle," for neither Dr. Shinn nor I intend to relinquish the right or duty to speak to particular action or legislation.

To draw once again on the World Order Study Conference at St. Louis for illustration, I would suggest that the churchmen there assembled (including of course both laymen and clergy) knew full well the implications and possible—*I* believe probable—consequences in Vietnam of urging negotiations, a cessation of bombing, and phased withdrawal of American troops "to be replaced by adequate international peace-keeping forces." Tucked away in separate unconnected Reports, which were "received" but not "approved" by the conference, lay these sentences: "Some form of Communist or other authoritarian society may seem to be the best practical option available in a particular historic situation.[4] ... Our support for democratic institutions and our anticommunist convictions should not compromise our belief in the right of a people to determine the form of government best suited to its time and needs.[5] ... We urge our own government not to seek to impose our economic or political system on all nations.[6] ... We must not let our fervor for anti-Communism outweigh our dedication to social justice for all peoples."[7]

I am not here arguing the truth or error of these assertions. I *am* suggesting that they represent a Christian critique of American ideology, but hidden as background information and probably unknown to most of those who will castigate the National Council of Churches (erroneously) for the conference's alleged (but distorted) recommendation of "withdrawal from Vietnam." Incidentally, the conference also spent considerable time debating—and condemning—the Selden Resolution on hemispheric intervention, to which Dr. Shinn referred. I wish I could be as sure as he is, however, that "*everybody knew* that the resolution had no legal force and that it was worded so vaguely as to justify practically any kind of intervention." Latin Americans did not know it—or believe that we know it. I am not sure that all of our Congressmen knew it. Although some of them have admitted that it represented diplomatic horse-trading or an *im*pure act of piety ("sheer paganism or malignant heresy," as Dr. Shinn so aptly called it), but at least one Congressman at St. Louis spoke heatedly as if the conference criticism were a personal vendetta against Mr. Selden or the entire United States Congress.

All I am trying to say is that we have done a very poor job so far of justifying before the American public, Christian or non-Christian, our theological critique or national ideologies—a critique on which our advocacy of specific policies must be based. Or perhaps we simply need to make explicit for the public what is implicit but clear to theologians who presume to speak on social issues.

As those of you involved with the student generation well know, "the idolatry of law and order as the ultimate criteria of moral action" poses an immediate crisis within the Christian community and outside. In a report on the World Order Study Conference I commented that the right of dissent appeared to me the one substantially new element at St. Louis, attested to by its inclusion in three of the five topical sections. The conference said: "Christians have the duty to dissent when their basic convictions are contradicted by governmental policy and be willing to bear the consequences of their dissent." An attempt to insert the phrase "by legal means" was defeated! But the group also affirmed that "the right of dissent should be expressed with responsibility both to the integrity of the individual conscience and to the common good."

It is at this point that I would raise two final questions for Dr. Shinn:

1. Is there not a real tension between the admonition never to "let the laws of society become the final definition of obedience to God" and the immediately following warning about perverted individualism? Regardless of what alternative forms of service are offered (or the willingness of some dissenters to fight for the United Nations or in privately chosen "just wars"), the demand for *selective* conscientious objection, based not on pacifism or any other universal principle, presents a painful dilemma for ethics and theology.

2. In the light of the Supreme Court decision of March, 1965, that a conscientious objector need not affirm a theistic faith, what is the public responsibility of theology toward a still more selective conscience which is *not* itself rooted in theology? Or, in other words, does theology have an obligation to defend "nontheological"—or at least nontheistic—ethics; and if so, how? In one sense, this brings us full circle to the initial problem raised; namely, whether the so-called "new morality" and "new theology" stand in a new relationship to each other, to the world, and to "God."

I am sincerely grateful for the opportunity to have retangled Dr. Shinn's neat and thought-provoking world, if only to push one of our ablest ethical scholars farther toward a theology of public responsibility.

NOTES

1. Sixth World Order Study Conference, *Final Report*, mimeographed October 23, 1965, "Section III, Addenda," p. 3. The final printed form was not available at the time of writing.

2. *Ibid.,* "Recommendations, Section III," p. 7.

3. Cf. Harvey Cox, "New Phase in the Marxist-Christian Encounter," *Christianity and Crisis,* November 1, 1965, pp. 226–230.

4. Sixth World Order Study Conference, *Draft Report,* Section III, p. 2. This sentence was edited out, but not voted out, of the *Final Report.*

5. *Final Report,* Section III, p. 5.

6. *Ibid.,* p. 2.

7. *Ibid.,* p. 3.